Tough
Choices
Young Women Talk
about Pregnancy
**Alison Hadley of
Brook, editor**

Brook
putting young people first

Livewire

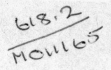

618.2

MOUL65

First published by Livewire Books, The Women's Press Ltd, 1999
A member of the Namara Group
34 Great Sutton Street, London EC1V 0LQ

British Library Cataloguing-in-Publication Data
A catalogue record for this book is available from the British Library.

ISBN 0 7043 4953 1

Typeset in 12/14pt Bembo by FSH Ltd, London
Printed and bound in Great Britain by Cox & Wyman Ltd, Reading,
Berkshire

Acknowledgements

I would like to thank all the young women who have contributed to this book and the many others whose stories I did not have room to include. Their openness in sharing their stories will help many teenagers with their thoughts and decisions about pregnancy. Thanks too to my editing partners Helen Windrath and Nancy Pickford for helping to preserve the individuality of each contribution, and to all those in Brook who supported my belief that the story of teenage pregnancy needs to be told by the young women themselves.

Contents

Introduction

When you're young, thinking you might be pregnant can be really scary – so scary that sometimes it's tempting to blame a missed period on stress and try to pretend everything is normal. When you do pluck up the courage to go to the doctor or a clinic for a pregnancy test, or to buy a home kit, you then have the nerve-racking wait for the result. If it's positive, you're suddenly faced with a million things to think about. Who is it safe to tell? How will they react? And what decision are you going to make about the pregnancy? Finding out that you're pregnant feels like life will never be the same again.

Every year in Britain, 100,000 young women go through this experience, 10 per cent of them while they're not yet 16. For the vast majority the pregnancy is completely unplanned.

People often find it hard to believe that young women can get pregnant from lack of knowledge! But every day at

Brook we see young women having to deal with an unplanned pregnancy simply because no one gave them the information they needed. We may be bombarded with sex all the time – in magazines, films and ice-cream ads – but we rarely get proper sex education. Many teenagers get pregnant, for example, because they don't know about emergency (after sex) contraception or that they can get free and confidential contraceptive advice even if they are under 16. I hope the Factfile (page 111) answers some of the most common questions and Brook will always give advice either over the phone or at one of our centres around the UK.

But while the causes of teenage pregnancy don't often make the headlines, the media can be very critical of young women who do get pregnant. If you decide to have your baby you risk being accused of deliberately becoming pregnant to get a council flat. On the other hand, if you choose abortion because you don't feel ready to bring up a child, you may be called irresponsible and selfish.

What we rarely hear are the voices of the young women themselves, so it was great to be asked to compile this collection of first-hand accounts. At last, young women can talk about their experiences in their own words, without the 'spin' of the media. Other teenagers also have the chance of hearing what it's really like to be pregnant young.

I am very grateful to the contributors for telling their stories with such honesty. They have vividly described their emotional and practical ups and downs in a way that gives us a very personal view of their lives. Some stories were painful to read, others very positive, but what was so striking was that none fits the stereotype of the pregnant teenager we so often hear about.

Being a teenage mother is not the inevitable disaster it's painted to be. Even though most of the contributors who had their babies wish they had been older, all of them are doing well. Although life is not easy, many of them have passed their exams and started courses or jobs. Of those who had abortions, none of them made their decision lightly, but even with the sadness they experienced they felt that their choice was the right one. What struck me most though, was how seriously the young women took the responsibility of making their choices and their strength and courage in living with those decisions.

I really hope that this collection of personal accounts will help to open up the subject of teenage pregnancy and make it easier for young women to ask for advice. Many of the young women in this book found it really difficult to tell anyone about their pregnancy. Some were so worried about their parents' anger or disappointment that they didn't say anything for several months. A few were so afraid that they concealed their pregnancies almost until they gave birth.

At Brook we believe that the only person who can make the final decision about a pregnancy is the young woman herself and that she should be supported in whatever choice she makes. But we also know that the more opportunities there are to discuss the pros and cons of being pregnant young, the easier it will be for young women to make the choices that are right for them.

So many thanks once again to all the young women in this book who have had to make those tough choices. I believe that their courage in sharing their stories will help many other young people in the future.

Alison Hadley of Brook

I Haven't Looked Back

I'd just split up with my boyfriend Dave when I discovered I was pregnant. I was 17. I'd been on the pill previously but had come off it following a news scare. We'd used a condom but it had split. I naïvely assumed that I wouldn't get pregnant so didn't even consider going to the doctor's for the morning-after pill.

All was forgotten for a month or so until my period was a couple of weeks late. I remember sitting in my German class at school. I had a gut feeling that I was pregnant; I could just sense it. I confided in my best friend and we decided to get a pregnancy test after school. I was so scared waiting for the results. The two blue lines confirmed my worst nightmare – I was pregnant.

I felt so alone. I couldn't tell my mum, she'd go mad. She didn't really get on with Dave and she had high expectations of me. I felt I'd let her down badly and I knew she'd be really disappointed. I phoned up Dave. We were still very close and I hoped he would understand. He was really supportive and we discussed the situation. I had my A levels in four months and wanted to go to university that year. We both agreed that we were too young to have a child.

Stupidly I told another of my so-called friends, who proceeded to tell people in the sixth form. The gossip soon spread around the whole school and I was constantly being pointed and stared at. I hated it.

I decided, after a lot of crying sessions with Dave, to have an abortion. We felt we didn't have enough to offer a child. We had to do so much sneaking around behind my mum's back. I had to skive school to attend checkups at the abortion clinic and doctor's. I felt so dirty and guilty for lying to the person closest to me.

One day things came to a head. I was supposed to be at my weekend job but had an appointment with my doctor. My mum came to see me at work and was concerned when I wasn't there. She was told I'd phoned in sick and got a bit angry when I wasn't at home either. When I returned later, she started shouting at me. I knew I had to tell her the truth. I just blurted it out: 'I'm pregnant but I've sorted it all out. I'm going to have an abortion.' I deliberately mentioned the abortion in the same breath so my mum wouldn't be too disappointed. She went silent. Then she came and sat next to me and put her arm around me. For the first time I felt immense relief and I knew everything was going to be okay.

We talked for ages and she said she would support me whatever my decision. I'd thought she would go mad but she was great and the biggest support ever. I wasn't that close to my dad as my parents had split up when I was young. But I decided to tell him, and he was fine about it.

I had an abortion about three weeks later. Although I occasionally stop and think when I see a baby, I haven't looked back. I split up for good with Dave about nine months ago. The abortion was nearly three and a half years ago.

I am now an air stewardess, which I really enjoy and I have never been happier. I would just like to express my regret at not telling my mum when I first found out that I was pregnant. One of the worst things about everything was keeping it secret from her. I realise now that parents can be a real support and it's better to involve them as soon as you're in trouble.

Julia Baynton

We've Come Through

I met my boyfriend during a drunken night at a local pub. I was 16, he was 18. We got together and instinctively knew that we were right for each other. For seven months everything was perfect, until we found out I was pregnant. Right from the start I knew that I was pregnant but funnily enough neither of us was particularly bothered. We'd been going out for such a short time, but it seemed like for ever and we were in love.

At the time things were a little strained between me and my parents – typical teenage rebellion – and I couldn't face telling them. I felt such a failure, that I'd let down them down so badly. I sat and cried, not at the thought of being pregnant but at having to tell Mum and Dad that I'd mucked up my life.

My boyfriend and I waited until the doctor confirmed the pregnancy and then we faced my parents together. I just walked in and said, 'I've got something to tell you and you're not going to like it, but I'm pregnant.' They both sat there, my dad's eyes boring into me and my mum in tears. It was the worst moment of my life.

I made it clear that my boyfriend was standing by me and there was no way I was getting rid of our baby. Mum and Dad were actually really good about it, although they stressed that it would be in everybody's interest if I didn't have it. They admitted they knew that I would keep it anyway because I'm so stubborn. Dad was more talkative than Mum. I felt really guilty because she was so upset. I'd spoilt all their hopes for me.

My boyfriend and I talked it through. We both agreed without doubt that I would have this baby, no matter what anybody said. The next few days at home were tense. Mum wouldn't speak to me and Dad was very standoffish. Eventually Mum and I had a massive argument and I left home to live with my boyfriend and his mum. We put our names on the council waiting list but were told not to expect much as the list was very long.

I spent the next three months depressed. Again, it wasn't about the baby – I knew that I'd cope (I'd been doing a nursery nursing course that I'd had to give up) – but about being cut off from my parents. Dad would phone occasionally but Mum wouldn't speak to me. I didn't see any friends from school, only my sister, who popped up when she was in the area, and two close friends. I must have spent the whole time crying. Thinking about it now, it should have driven me and my partner apart, but it brought us even closer.

We were eventually offered a council flat in a nice area. It was perfect. Suddenly there was light at the end of the tunnel. It was a new start, a clean break. Mum even started to talk to me again. Everything was working out. We moved in and had great fun decorating. My pride and joy was the baby's room. It had to be perfect. Everybody gave us furniture and household bits. I finally felt I was being accepted. Mum even offered to take me to the doctor's for check-ups and to hospital. My boyfriend and I were really happy, even though we were so young and didn't know what we were getting into.

Three months later, after a very painful 22-hour labour, I gave birth to a baby boy. We called him Daniel. The amount of presents and cards we received was amazing. We were swamped.

The sleepless nights were a strain on us, but not on our relationship. We managed remarkably well. Money was the only problem. Living on one small wage wasn't easy. We were always short of something. We had very worrying times – when the bills came in, when the car needed taxing and insuring – but we always managed to scrape through. Mum and Dad turned out to be amazing, helping us whenever they could. We couldn't have got through it without their support.

Daniel is nearly five now, and we have a daughter, Robyn, who is almost three. It hasn't been easy and we've had our ups and downs but we've come through. We've surprised an awful lot of people by staying together for over six years and we've never been happier.

My advice to anybody in the same position is to go with your instincts. If you are completely sure that you can love and look after your child, and you know you will have support, then go for it. But be sure you know what you're doing. It's hard work, especially if you're young, and you have to put everything else on hold. No more nights out or wild drunken parties. We usually get out together about once every three months, but it's enough for us. We enjoy spending all our time with the children.

Looking back, it was the wrong time for us to have a child and we would have preferred to wait. But these things happen, and I wouldn't change my children for the world. Seeing them discover new things, walk, talk and laugh, is enough to prove that.

Julie Cruickshank

She's So Lovely

I think I knew I was pregnant even before I missed my first period, even though I had always practised safe sex by using condoms. I was with my boyfriend when I took a home pregnancy test and both our reactions were of pure shock. I don't think either one could quite believe it. After the second test also showed positive, however, we knew we had to look at the situation realistically.

I was in my gap year before university. My boyfriend and I had only been together for about six months, but we had already announced our engagement. I think this made it easier to discuss what to do, as we were secure in our relationship and knew that whatever the decision, we would work through it together. We discussed it for about three months before we told anyone I was pregnant. We had still not reached a final decision about keeping the baby.

Telling my mum was the hardest thing I have ever

done in my entire life. She was desperately disappointed and discussed all the options with me. She knew I had a place at university and had got a good job in my gap year. She would rather I pursued a career and waited to have a baby later on in life.

I discussed my pregnancy with many people – my family, my boyfriend's family and our friends – and took on board everything they said, good and bad. I think coming to a decision was made easier by me living independently in my own flat, which meant I did not feel under pressure from my parents. My boyfriend was very keen for me to have the baby but he also understood that the final decision had to be mine, as I was making the biggest sacrifice and would have to put both my education and career on hold.

I think a big part of my decision to keep the baby was helped by knowing that although it would be a massive financial struggle, my boyfriend would support me and we would never go without or have to rely on the welfare system. When I announced my final decision to keep the baby, most people's reactions were very positive. My mum said she would support me even though she did not agree with my choice.

I don't think my doctor treated me as well as she could. She was quite flippant and seemed not to take me too seriously. She hardly explained anything to me, such as booking antenatal classes. The hospital staff, however, were brilliant and treated me with the utmost respect, rather than just 'another teenage pregnancy'.

I had an absolutely brilliant pregnancy – no morning sickness, dizziness, swollen ankles – and I managed to work as an assistant manager of a bar right up to three weeks before my baby was due. I felt very emotional a lot of the time, as you swing from excitement to immense and over-whelming panic about what the future holds and whether your baby will be completely healthy and perfect.

I thoroughly enjoyed being pregnant and cherished every movement the baby made. I watched in amazement as my stomach grew and as I saw the developing baby on the scans and thought about the life I had created. I think the scariest thought was that this child was going to be totally reliant on me and would have nothing except what I could give her. She would be wholly vulnerable and dependent and I would be the only one to make sure she was safe and loved.

When I went two weeks over my due date, I was admitted into hospital to have my baby induced. I was worried, but at least I knew exactly when the baby was coming and could prepare myself. My labour lasted about five and a half hours. It was relatively easy as I opted to have an epidural, which was fantastic. And my boyfriend and my mum were with me, which was a great support. Jenny was born on 23 March at 8.24 p.m. She weighed eight pounds six ounces and she was utterly perfect.

After the birth, despite being exhausted, I felt exhilarated and had an unexplainable surge of love for my child. It was only when I went home the next morning that it hit me that I was actually a mother. My new daughter absolutely fascinated me. I found everything she did amazing – and still do!

At first I found it very hard to adjust. Suddenly I had no spare time, not enough sleep and someone completely dependent on me. Eventually I relaxed and Jenny and I started to learn and develop a relationship together. I was lucky in that my baby is very good and after six weeks she started sleeping through the night. I was also very lucky to have so much support from my family, my partner and his family, and all our friends, which helped prevent me suffering from postnatal depression.

My boyfriend took two weeks' holiday when we came back from hospital, which was great as he completely took over everything: cleaning, cooking and entertaining our mountains of visitors. We had a lovely time together and all three of us got to know each other as a family. It was hard adjusting when he went back to work, as he works both days and nights in the entertainment industry. My friends were good to me but when the novelty wore off so did their involvement. I still see them but mainly on their holidays, as most of them are at uni.

I don't think I've encountered any problems yet being a teenage mum. I would like to get out more in the evenings but, to be honest, my baby gives me more pleasure than sitting in a pub or clubbing. I still manage to go shopping or go for lunch or coffee. The only thing that's quite restricting is having to breastfeed all the time but, again, you learn to adjust. One good thing about being a teenage mother is that you are a bit more relaxed and willing to accept advice and help, which I'm sure makes you and your baby happier. Being younger means you have more energy. You and your baby can learn together and watch each other grow as people.

In my case the good times definitely outweigh the bad. Every time Jenny smiles I feel all my hard work has paid off. My hopes for the future, apart from making my daughter as happy as I can, are to take up my university place, get my degree and maybe go into teaching or counselling. Whatever I decide to do, my hope is that my boyfriend, my baby and I will all remain happy and safe and I can become not only a mother and a friend to my daughter but also a role model.

Jane Clark

Not Just a Working-Class Condition

I had just turned 16 when I fell pregnant. I spent weeks in complete shock. I was in my last year of high school, about to sit my GCSEs and with plans to go to college. My boyfriend and I hadn't been together very long at all. When I broke the news to him, he said if I decided to keep the baby, he would support me all he could. I had no reason to doubt this as he was 24 and I knew he had another son whom he saw regularly and supported financially.

After many sleepless nights I decided to keep my baby. I mistakenly thought that the baby would have a mother and a father to raise him as best as they could. In fact, my boyfriend left me when I was four and a half months pregnant.

I had a lot of support from my mum, after the initial shock. Although my dad accepted my decision to keep the baby, he wouldn't discuss it. If anyone mentioned my pregnancy or the approaching birth, he would go very quiet and pretend to be watching TV or something. I also received an awful lot of support from my high school – from my head of year and deputy head in particular – both with the pregnancy and my GCSE exams, which I sat (and passed) when I was five months pregnant.

I spent the summer getting everything I needed for my baby. I was still living at home with my mum and dad and older sister. Towards the end of my pregnancy I attended antenatal classes for teenage mums at my local hospital. I found this really relaxing because I wasn't in a room full of 30-something couples, all married for years with fantastic careers.

My son Joe was born on 25 November at 7.30 a.m., after a short 3-hour labour, weighing 9 pounds and 11 ounces. My mum was with me at the birth. I've only seen his father once since; he came to visit when Joe was 18 months old. He doesn't pay any child support.

Since having Joe, my life has changed a lot. I still do things that my friends do, such as go clubbing and to the cinema occasionally. My parents are brilliant when it comes to babysitting. They both love Joe very much. I have had a lot of support from my friends and family. I'm very lucky in that respect.

When Joe was nine months old, I started my A levels. Two years later I passed and last year I decided to move and start a degree at university. It was incredibly hard work and unfortunately I only lasted one term. I think maybe I should have waited until Joe started school.

Being a single teenage mum wasn't something I ever thought would happen to me. Single teenage mums are stereotyped to be from working-class backgrounds with few, if any, academic qualifications – not bright, middle-class girls like myself. But it goes to show, anyone who isn't 100 per cent safe when it comes to sex can end up like me.

I am hoping to start my Project 2000 course next year to train as a nurse. I am now in a committed relationship with a man who has not only given both myself and Joe a lot of security, but has also helped me look towards a positive future.

Sara Earnshaw

The Last Straw

Last April when I was 16 I discovered any teenager's
worst nightmare. I was pregnant. Only a few months
earlier I had done a pregnancy test after being three
weeks late. Luckily it was negative. This time my mum
was getting ever more suspicious because I started getting
morning sickness and cravings. The thought of Super-
noodles suddenly made me feel violently sick, after being
mad for them before. That was the last straw. My mum
went and bought me a pregnancy test.

The result was supposed to take 2 minutes but after
only 30 seconds I had the shock of my life. It was
positive. My initial reaction was to burst into tears but I
felt numb. All I wanted was to be on my own. I also knew
I had to face my boyfriend, Tim. We had only been
together a few months.

I had always said if I ever fell pregnant I would have an

abortion, but I never expected it to be a reality. My mum insisted I had an abortion. She never even bothered asking me what I wanted. However, she was really calm. She didn't blame me, even though it had been me and my boyfriend's fault for having sexual intercourse for three months without protection. At that point I didn't know what I wanted. It hadn't even sunk in that I was pregnant. It was like one big, bad nightmare.

Telling Tim was easy. I knew he would understand. We'd talked about it before and he said he'd support me whatever my decision.

The next day Mum and I visited my local doctor, who booked me in at the health centre the following Monday to arrange an abortion. By this stage I was around seven or eight weeks pregnant. Friday came, and Mum and her boyfriend went off on holiday for a week. She didn't want to go but I insisted. I needed time to think about what was actually going on in my life and to gain control. Mum arranged for me to stay with one of her friends who is really nice and has a daughter my age.

I grew more and more confused as the days wore on and by Monday I was really nervous. At the health centre I was called into a little room where a doctor asked me lots of questions, such as my age and what me and my boyfriend's situation was. He asked me if we had used protection and I said yes. I knew this would save a lecture about diseases, etc. Then he gave me an internal examination. I felt really intimidated as a medical student stood and watched. It was after that that it suddenly sunk in. I had something growing inside me that may have a life ahead of it. I realised I needed some time to think. I was then booked in for an abortion at the centre the following day. I can't explain how I felt that day. It was strange and felt like an intimate nightmare.

When I got back I was petrified and refused to go the next day. The woman I was staying with rearranged it for the week after, when my mum would be home. I cried for days in confusion and hate: hate for my mum forcing me into an abortion and hate for myself for being so stupid.

Over the next five days before Mum got home I really thought about what was ahead of me. I still didn't know what to do. I was attempting to make the hardest decision of my life. I had to weigh up the pros and cons and decide what would be best for now and the future. After all, I was a lost 16-year-old with a 19-year-old boyfriend. I wasn't fully mature and certainly wasn't old enough to be responsible for another life as well as mine.

It was really hard for me as no one understood how I was feeling, apart from those who had been through it themselves. My mum was really supportive when I told her I was unsure about what I wanted. At the end of the day I had to do what was best for me and the baby. I finally decided to have an abortion. It would be best for everyone. I had to think about my future. I wanted to be a teacher. My exams were coming up and I knew there would be no way I could carry on doing A levels with a baby. I also knew Tim wasn't ready to be a father and I wasn't sure we'd always be together. It would have been selfish of me to keep the baby as I knew we couldn't have given it everything it would need.

The day of the abortion arrived. I was extremely nervous and still partly unsure in my mind, but I knew I was doing the right thing. Well, not necessarily the *right* thing, but the *best* thing. At the health centre a nurse talked to me to make me aware of what was involved and I signed a form of consent. Everything was so unreal. To the nurses and doctors I was just another patient that had made a mistake. It was nothing to them. They didn't care that I was petrified of what was about to happen.

The nurse placed a pessary inside me to start my cervix softening, which would make the abortion process easier. It gave me chronic stomach cramp. At that point I wished I was anywhere but there. Mum sat at my bedside the whole time. About three hours later I was then taken to another room and given a general anaesthetic. Tears came to my eyes as I was wheeled away from Mum. The nurses and doctors seemed to show no sympathy. I felt insulted by what they might have thought of me.

The next thing I knew, I was awake and crying from the anaesthetic. I dropped off again with Mum comforting me and then woke a bit later, feeling dreadful. I was bleeding slightly and wearing a massive sanitary towel. Mum had to support me when I got dressed and went home, as I felt so dizzy and didn't have the energy to walk. I felt no discomfort from the operation, just tired and depressed.

A few weeks later, I wasn't coping too well. The pill I was put on was giving me headaches and depression. A day didn't go by when I didn't cry. I couldn't go on like it, so Mum booked me an appointment at the family planning clinic. They changed my pill and booked me in to see a counsellor at the health centre. The woman I saw was really nice. I was so relieved to share my problems with someone who wouldn't judge me. We not only talked about my abortion, but also about my parents splitting up a year before, my exams and my relationship with my mum (we never really got on). Seeing the counsellor helped enormously. After a month, I realised I had come to terms with a lot of things.

The day of my abortion was the worst day of my life and one I shall never forget. I have learnt to cope with what happened, but even six months later, I still had bad days, and many things would upset me, such as seeing young mothers pushing their prams.

Over two years have passed now since my abortion. Life is very different. My boyfriend and I didn't last; neither did my A level plans. I'm currently working in a factory and doing an evening computer class. I plan to become a legal secretary one day. My relationship with my mum has grown somewhat since I moved out of home and things are looking up for me.

I would really like a baby, more than anything in the world, but I will wait until the time is right. Looking back, I see how immature my boyfriend and I both were for not using protection, and I realise I made the right decision for me at that time. After all, I still have the future ahead of me!

Rachel Griffiths

Stubborn as a Mule

I was 17 and working when I found out that I was pregnant. I was living in a care home at the time and one night I came home plastered out of my head because of an argument with my dad. My boyfriend Stuart, who lived in the same care home, helped me to my bed and then basically helped himself.

I'd never really been drunk before. The snogging and stuff was all very nice, especially after being told by my dad that I was a slut and he never wanted to see me again. Suddenly somebody wanted me and I didn't really care who it was. I remember resisting the sex bit for a while but then I was too wrecked to do anything after that.

I woke up the next day and tried to remember what had happened. It was like a nightmare. I couldn't believe that Stuart would do something like that to me, after all I'd told him. I ended the relationship with him that day but I carried on loving him for ever.

I was terrified of letting anyone know. I was quite naive and I'd had sex in my bedroom, a cardinal sin at the care home. I didn't do anything for weeks but I knew I was pregnant. I had to be; no one would let me be lucky enough to get away with it.

I eventually put a pregnancy test in to my GP. It seemed for ever until I got my results. I went alone. I was so scared of what people would think of me that I still hadn't told anyone. It was the loneliest feeling I'd had in a long time. The receptionist at the surgery was really nice. She took me into their little staffroom and went to check my results. The minute she walked back in I knew she was going to tell me something I wasn't going to like. The test was positive. The next thing I knew I was on the floor in her arms.

They wouldn't let me go home on my own and called my social worker to come and collect me. It was finally out in the open. I remember the question: do you know what your options are? I had been a virgin up until then and had never wanted to have sex. I couldn't even begin to think about my options. All I knew was that this was probably the biggest and most traumatic thing I would ever have to deal with.

My key worker at the home was very supportive. She sat down with me and told me what options I had but said it was up to me which choice I made. She was always there for me and never judged me for what had happened.

I never felt that abortion was an option. I don't know why, but it felt like I'd be killing something that shared no blame of what had happened. I did, however, consider adoption. It was a really difficult decision to make. I was torn between not wanting to be like my mother and proving that I could do better than her. I guess from my family's point of view my pregnancy was just what they had been expecting. I was just another 'tart' who would sooner or later get into trouble.

For about six weeks I couldn't stop crying. I stayed out of everyone's way, especially my ex-boyfriend's. I was throwing up all the time and lost a lot of weight. The staff at the home tried really hard to keep my spirits up; sometimes they were successful and other times they weren't.

Before long I lost my job, as I kept passing out at work and throwing up. The letter they wrote was very polite and carefully didn't indicate my pregnancy as the reason for letting me go (you can't get sacked for being pregnant). This was yet another blow to recover from – yet I did.

The appointment to discuss fostering and adoption was drawing near and I could feel myself becoming more nervous as the days went by. On the day I sat in the staff office, waiting for everyone to arrive, and suddenly said to my key worker that I didn't want to give the baby up. She cancelled the appointment. I suddenly realised that if I'd given it away, I would have felt like a failure – not necessarily to myself but to my baby. I wanted to prove to myself that I was nothing like my mother. For the first time in my life I had control over what was happening to me. No one was going to make this choice for me – they couldn't. This thing was growing inside *me*.

My ex-boyfriend then found out about the baby. I hadn't told him because I was too angry at him. He was now sleeping with someone else in the home – someone

I'd made the mistake of confiding in – and she'd told him. He just thought he was really clever and started spreading all sorts of stuff about me.

I became very volatile and got angry easily. I ended up shouting at a woman who was looking at me in a baby shop. At that moment I realised what I was to everyone: another single mother who would probably drain the welfare system for the rest of my life and waste honest tax-payers' money. I could imagine her thinking that people like me should be made to have an abortion or give up the baby for adoption. But I was as stubborn as a mule and had no intention of letting them take away my control.

I had a huge struggle getting any benefits because I'd been sacked. I had to write to my MP twice. I was clinging on by the skin of my teeth to stay in reality and not drift into some world where anything was better than what I was going through.

Physically the pregnancy was a nightmare. I was vomiting and passing out, as well as having very severe pains in my stomach. I had to go into hospital quite often for up to six hours, and they would monitor everything. Once, when I was seven months pregnant, a ward sister came up to me and told me that the only reason I was in there was because I was pregnant. Otherwise they wouldn't bother with people like me. It made me feel like a complete inconvenience. I was 17 and very scared. I was still a kid who wanted to do all the things my friends were doing: rock climbing, trampolining, playing volleyball. The outcome of my numerous scans was that I had gallstones, which was quite rare at my age.

Every antenatal appointment was an effort; all those women with husbands or partners, and me with my key worker. Then there was a complication with the pregnancy. A scan revealed there was not enough fluid around the baby to allow it to grow properly. Continuing the pregnancy to the full nine months could have resulted in a stillbirth, so they set a date to induce the birth.

At the hospital, they started the induction by inserting cream inside me. After a night of extremely painful contractions, without any support, my social worker arrived (she stayed with me right up to the birth), and a consultant. He asked me if I'd had a comfortable night. What a joke! I'd had a night of agony and I told him this. His initial attitude was very much 'yet another stupid 17-year-old – what would she know about pain?' But after examining me, he sent me immediately up to the delivery suite, where my waters were broken and I was given an epidural. They eventually told me I could do some 'practice pushing'. When the epidural had worn off a bit, I could push for real. I remember thinking, 'Worn off a bit? I don't think so!' After almost 24 hours of labour, I wasn't about to let myself be tortured by childbirth. I pushed hard and gave birth to a beautiful baby girl weighing in at seven pounds and nine ounces.

Breastfeeding was really painful. After four nights my breasts were so sore they were bleeding. I asked for a nipple shield and was told that sore nipples was the price for not keeping my legs shut. I was furious and very hurt. After seven days I was ready to go home.

Motherhood was not at all how I'd expected. Throughout my pregnancy I had been worried about not loving the baby the way a mother should, but I was told that I'd 'just click'. Well, I didn't 'just click'. I struggled for about six months before the bonding with my daughter happened. The problem was nothing to do with her as a baby; it was more to do with the circumstances of my pregnancy.

It was really hard adjusting to being a single mother. There were no nights out and I was lonelier than ever. My social life was a disaster. Every man I met saw me as an easy target – but I wasn't. I never wanted sex again.

But here I am, six years down the line, married with two beautiful daughters and planning a third (and final!) baby. It has never been easy and there have been so many hurdles to overcome, but with strength and belief in yourself you can do it.

Looking back, I would have preferred to wait to have sex, never mind a baby. I'm 23 and only now living the youth I never had. Sex brings so much baggage with it, my advice is to make sure the guy is really worth it. My oldest daughter doesn't remember her natural father and has only seen him three times in six years. He now has four children with three different women.

Being a single mother was tough but I know I made the best choice. I love my children and I'm grateful for the love they have for me. When they tell me I'm the best mum ever I know they aren't lying and that gives me the warmest, most loving feeling anyone could ever know.

Jayne Short

You Can't Change Things

When I found out I was pregnant I decided not to tell anyone. I was 16 and I wanted to make the decision about what to do on my own, without anyone else's opinion. I finally decided an abortion was the right choice. By this stage I was four months pregnant.

Up to that point I thought I'd been coping very well. It wasn't until after the abortion that I started to lose control. For three years I sat and wallowed in my own depression. I felt disgusted with myself. I even tried to become pregnant again, to replace the baby I aborted and prove to myself that I could be a good mother. Looking back I was stupid, but that's how the depression got to me.

Once, at a party, a friend of Shaun's (the baby's father) came up to me and asked if I was the one that had killed Shaun's baby. This was one and a half years after the abortion. That was the lowest point for me. It was impossible to forget what had happened, when people kept reminding me all the time.

That night I went home and told my mum all about it. This was when things started becoming easier. The guilt I'd carried for so long finally seemed easier to bear, but I still had a long way to go. So I started to go to counselling. At one point I was shown a letter from a woman who felt her abortion had destroyed her life. Even the children she now had reminded her of the aborted baby. There and then I decided that I did not want to feel that way in 20 years' time. I suddenly realised that the past was the past. No matter how hard you wished, you could never change things. It made me take a long, hard look at myself.

I started writing some poems, as this seemed a good way to admit how I felt. I cried when I wrote them, so they must have helped me come to terms with my feelings. What I'd like other girls in the same situation to understand is that it's not an easy choice, but you have to make the right one for yourself. Even if it seems 'wrong', it's right for you. The pain and the guilt do become easier to cope with if you work at it.

It's now been four years since the abortion. The anniversary of my baby's death went by recently without me even noticing, for the first time in all these years, and this was when I finally realised that my life can go on.

Claire-Marie Green

'You're Going to be a Grandma'

I was 15 years old when I fell pregnant and 16 when I had my son. I'd been seeing Rob for nearly two years and we were getting on very well, so I thought I would sleep with him. We didn't use any contraception as I thought it wouldn't happen to me on my first time.

A few months afterwards I started feeling ill and drained, so I went to the doctor's. He said he would do a pregnancy test and I just laughed at him and said, 'That's a waste of time, I'm not pregnant.' He said he'd do one anyway, to be on the safe side.

A week later the doctor told me I was nearly three months pregnant. I had to look at the results to see for myself. I walked out of the doctor's as if I'd just seen aliens. I sat in the park in a total daze, numb with shock. My emotions were running wild: I didn't know if I was happy or sad, excited or what.

I wasn't getting on with my mum or stepdad. I walked over to where Mum worked and just said, 'You're going to be a grandma,' and walked out. That night when I got home she was waiting for me. She sat me down and asked me what I was going to do. I told her I had to keep it; I'd had sex and would have to pay the consequences. Rob loved me and he'd said he'd look after me and the baby. Mum tried to tell me he might just be saying that, but I was convinced he loved me.

My friends all thought I was silly having a baby at my age. All they were concerned about was that boys wouldn't look at us if one of us was pushing a pram. But at my hospital visits the staff were all right and didn't judge me.

I felt so isolated and alone. I couldn't get my head around what was going on. Rob told me he loved me and was going to stay with me but it was all too much to take in. In the end we split up when I was four months pregnant, because he had love bites on his neck and I knew I didn't do them.

On my 16th birthday I left home and moved into a mother and baby unit. Being 16, pregnant and on my own was really scary. I just kept thinking, I'm all alone. The nearer the baby's due date got, the worse I felt. I asked my mum to be at the birth, so I'd have someone there for me.

I was in labour for six hours, which wasn't too bad. It didn't hurt as much as everyone had said, but it was just as scary as I'd expected. But it was brilliant holding the baby. It was an unreal feeling. I kept thinking, this is my baby!

It was quite scary when we got home, as the baby was so small and depended on me for everything. It was quite hard at first but I soon got used to all the responsibility. My school friends kept telling me to leave Joshua, my baby, at home with Mum so we could go out, but I just couldn't. It's easier now because I'm 18 and have made some good friends who also have children.

Rob still lives locally but hasn't come round to see Joshua at all. If he sees us in the street he just walks past. I sometimes feel quite bitter about him, but I'm not looking for another relationship; I just want to concentrate on Joshua and getting a job. It's not easy sharing myself with anyone else.

I'm living in my own flat now and I've just done a college course. I'm hoping for a permanent job working with young offenders and drug users. Some people think you get a house and all this money, but you don't even get enough to live on – certainly not enough for nice clothes or luxuries. But it's not all bad. You get lots of rewards as well. It gets easier as you get used to it. I wouldn't change a thing now. I'm enjoying every minute of being a teenage mother.

Marianne Lacey

Everything to Me

I was 15 when I got pregnant and I had my son at 16. I had a feeling I was pregnant because I didn't come on and I was feeling tired, sleeping all the time. I'd been seeing my boyfriend for about a year. I knew about sex education but I didn't really think about it at the time.

My choice to have my son was made easier because I was already three months pregnant when I found out. At first, my boyfriend tried to persuade me not to go ahead with the pregnancy, but there was no way I was having my baby terminated. I don't believe in abortion so I wouldn't have had one anyway, even if I wasn't so far gone. I felt that the baby was already part of me.

My dad was very supportive. My mum couldn't believe it at first. She didn't even know I was having sex so it was a double shock – she went mad! She was furious with my boyfriend, who was 24. She took him to the police and they prosecuted him for having underage sex – he spent a short time in prison.

Mum stayed with me all the way. Everyone was great, even my friends, but my mum felt that my boyfriend should have been more responsible. He said he would be there for me and the baby, but after the prosecution we split up. I can see now that he was just taking advantage of me and didn't care about me at all. He hasn't once visited to see his son.

I felt down when we first split up, but then I started to think about my baby and to plan things for when the baby came.

I felt so happy when I saw my newborn baby. It made me feel good about my decision to keep it.

I'm a lone parent now, and do everything – absolutely everything – for my son. I am very close to him and I wouldn't be without him. He has changed my views on life: I have a more positive outlook now and I also have goals that I hope to achieve.

At the moment, I have a part-time job and my son goes to nursery. Being pregnant interrupted my education and I hope to go back to college this September to do my GCSEs. I then want to do a GNVQ in health and social care. I'm definitely not planning any more children until I have got myself sorted out. Now is the time to develop my career.

I will be giving my son early sex education so that he can be a good example and make a man of himself. Having a child isn't just about dressing them up and pushing them around the streets. Kids need a lot of attention and it's very difficult when you're young and on your own. I get loads of support from my mum. Sadly my dad died last year and I really miss him and all the help he gave me. If I'd been in a flat on my own it would have been really tough.

The last three years have been really hard, but I'm a positive person and I know I can make something of my life.

Lucy Bond

Her Little Sister

I felt life had nothing worthwhile for me until I met Gary. I was very depressed because of severe bullying at school. Everyone called me a lesbian because I didn't have a boyfriend and wore glasses and wasn't attractive. I was also recovering from having a lump removed from my breast.

Within weeks, we moved into a flat together. Gary was 17 and I was 15. I had been taking the pill since I was 11 because of problem periods. I didn't realise it could also work as contraception and had stopped taking it for a few days when I was having my breast operation. I became pregnant and miscarried after 12 weeks. I carried on at school without anyone knowing I was living with Gary, but the loss of the baby shook me badly. Being pregnant had been a way of proving to myself that I had some worth in society.

By Christmas I had just got over the loss and was

concentrating on my forthcoming GCSEs. On Christmas day I was given the wishbone to pull with my brother. Everything went into slow motion as the bone snapped in half and I was left with the longer bit. I remember wishing that I wanted someone to love me for ever to give my life some meaning.

In January I started feeling sick, ill and tired. I knew deep down that something was wrong. My period was late but everyone said that was just due to the stress of the bullying at school.

I went to the family planning clinic with Gary, who waited outside. My whole body went numb as I watched the bright blue line appear on the tester. The doctor thought I had become pregnant because I'd been on antibiotics, which had stopped the pill being effective. We hadn't ever used condoms as we trusted each other and had been together for six months. I remember wondering what I was supposed to do now.

Gary's parents were really proud. It would be their first grandchild. I couldn't tell my parents. My mum had a baby really early in life and my dad wanted more of a life for me. They would have been disgusted and I was scared of rejection. When I still hadn't told my parents after two weeks, Gary's mum went with me to the doctor's to get it confirmed. I thought the doctor might try to put me off having the baby, but he said I was old enough and mature enough to have a healthy pregnancy.

When I finally told my mum I just hugged her and cried but we were both too scared to tell Dad. By the time I was 12 weeks pregnant everyone knew, even my school (thanks to Gary's sister boasting that she was going to be an aunty). All I had to do was tell my dad.

I remember standing in the kitchen when my dad walked in and said he needed to talk to me. I realised he must know. I tried to get away before he flew at me but then I just collapsed, sobbing. Instead of being angry, he stood there, hugging me. This was very unlike him; he had never shown me any affection before. We then sat down and talked. Dad was very calm and said he thought I'd be happier if I had an abortion. He offered me some money and said he'd arrange for me to have a termination privately. But he added that he'd stick by me whatever I did. He told me he felt guilty, that it was his fault we didn't have a bond any more.

I couldn't go through with an abortion. When I saw the first scan at 12 weeks I felt overwhelmed. It was a life inside me; I'd just lost one. Everyone promised to help me, saying that they'd be there for me and help with money. If only I'd known how hard the struggle would be.

Before my baby was born, Gary suddenly decided he didn't want to be with me any more and moved back in with his mum. I was desperately unhappy and it all became too much for me, what with the pregnancy, the bullying and now Gary leaving me. I'd already been seeing a counsellor because of the bullying and I ended up spending a few days in psychiatric care. All the fantasies of motherhood wore off and I decided to have my baby adopted by my sister.

After the birth I stayed with my sister for a few days and then she went away on holiday. Gary and I were back together again; I think he had just panicked before. We'd had problems with our flat and the landlord had locked us out, so we were staying in my sister's flat with the baby while she was away.

I didn't really feel anything for the baby, but I started breastfeeding him. It felt as though that was the only way I could give him love. We didn't have a bond straight away. I felt guilty about that, although now I know that lots of women feel like that. He was just a helpless baby. Even though I was his mother, I was helpless too. Every time I looked at him I felt I was looking at myself. He was now a part of me and that would never change. He was my son. I decided to keep him.

When my sister returned, she could see that I was coping well and took a step back. She hadn't particularly wanted to be his mother, but was trying to be supportive by offering to adopt him. She just wanted to help me – her little sister.

Suddenly I was homeless with a three-week-old baby. The council put me into temporary accommodation. I knew then there was no turning back.

I started college, doing a course in child and social development. Mathew, my baby, stayed with a childminder next to the college and I managed to breastfeed him throughout, which I feel quite proud about. For a long time I felt that I had to prove a point to everyone: I was a housewife, mother and student. If I failed at one of them it would have ruptured the whole chain. I wasn't anyone's little girl any more – that hurt the most, and still does.

Gary and I broke up when Mathew was two and a half, but he still sees him every fortnight. Our relationship was going nowhere and I wanted to see more of life. I'd never had any other relationships and I wanted to meet more people.

I'm 21 now and Mathew has just turned 4. I stopped

the college course when he was three, as I wanted to be a full-time mum. The guilt of having him so young will never leave me. I had nothing to offer him. He had to learn while I learned. I still feel particularly bad about letting down my dad, as he had high hopes for me. But he really loves Mathew and spends loads of time with him.

I don't feel as isolated now as I did before. Most of my friends have got children now as well. I don't have any bullying to cope with. My parents and my older sister have helped me a lot, and I've managed to keep up with all my interests. I feel now I have a wider perspective on life. I don't have a career, so I'm concentrating on me and Mathew. I want to build on our bond: I want to love him and love him and love him. I'm just lucky that I have a son like Mathew. He's everything I want in a child, so loving and understanding. He makes up the love for both of us.

I now live with Tim, someone I've known for some time. Last year I got pregnant, but we decided that I should have an abortion, as we realised how much harder it would be with two children. I knew straight away it wouldn't be right to have the baby and never really felt any bond, so having the abortion wasn't painful. I feel that it was a positive decision and have never regretted it. We're really happy together and now thinking about when would be a good time to have children together.

I suppose I want to live the stereotyped, white-picket-fence sort of life. Deep down I still need to feel proud of myself and stop feeling guilty.

Samantha Williams

Addicted to Love

I found out I was pregnant just before my 16th birthday. I knew I was pregnant because my belly started getting big when I was just a few weeks.

I couldn't believe it. I was completely shocked. I had talked about babies with my boyfriend, Carl, but we weren't planning to have any so soon. We hadn't been using condoms when I got pregnant because I'd been with my boyfriend for three years and I thought there was enough trust. I'd been taking the pill on and off, but I'd missed a few. I did a home pregnancy test that my boyfriend got for me and it came up positive. The doctor's confirmed it.

I told my boyfriend first and he was really happy; he's older than me and said he would support me. He told his mum straight away and she was very upset because I was so young. She didn't really want me to keep it.

It took me three weeks to tell my mum. I was really scared but once I told my mum it got even harder for a while. She was upset because I was so young and still in school and she wanted me to get more out of life.

I was going to have a termination but on the day my boyfriend and I decided against it. I thought I would regret it for the rest of my life. Once I had made the decision to keep my baby I enjoyed the rest of my pregnancy.

Things were hard, though, because my boyfriend went into prison when I was three months pregnant. Our relationship was always difficult. I'd been the one to chase Carl – I was addicted to him. He had a reputation as a hard nut and I thought he was wonderful, but I didn't see his full character. He was in and out of prison and was unfaithful at times as well. But he was being hassled about my age as I was only 12 when we started going out, and he was just trying to convince himself that he didn't care about me by seeing other girls. When we were alone in his flat, we got on well. We didn't have sex until later in the relationship.

When I told my friends that I was pregnant, most of them told me I shouldn't have it. They had children already so they knew how hard it was. But they said they would help in every way if I went ahead with the baby.

When I was in the hospital I was treated very badly. The staff were rude to my mother and made a comment about her not having any discipline over me and how terrible it was that I was having a baby when I was so young. They didn't show me any respect. The woman in the bed next to me was 30-something and had no problems at all.

My midwife was great, though, really nice. I couldn't have done it without her. As the birth got nearer I got really scared. What scared me most was the waiting and not knowing what to expect. When you ask people what it's like they all say different things.

When I went into labour I was in really bad pain. I just kept saying, 'I don't want to do it, I want to go home.' I was really horrible to my poor mum. I had two epidurals because the first didn't work. I don't know if I was more afraid of the needle or the pain. I also had pethidine, a pain-relieving drug.

The minute my baby, Max, was born I cried. The nurse took him to get measured and weighed and I started shouting, 'What are you doing with my baby!' I just wanted to hold that tiny baby that was mine and protect and love it. I couldn't wait to get out of bed and ring Carl. He was in prison at the time. When I did speak to him, I felt really alone and wanted him to be there to hold and feel proud of his baby.

When I took Max home I still lived with my mum so my stuff was all in one room. There were so many flowers, presents and cards everywhere. When I sat down that night I felt scared and tired and I almost wished I'd stayed in the hospital.

It was really weird trying to get used to my new life with a baby. Getting us both ready to leave the house took so much longer. Having responsibility for this tiny baby was really strange. It took me at least six months to feel like a real mum.

Carl was still in prison. It was hard for him because I couldn't do as much for him any more, because of Max, and he started to think that I didn't care. He felt I spent all my time with the baby and the baby didn't even know him. I felt bad to see how upset Carl was, not being able to get to know Max. But I also thought it wasn't fair that he had no responsibility and I was doing it all on my own – the sleepless nights and the shitty nappies.

I really wanted Carl to be a good, committed dad, but he found it quite hard. Prison doesn't help. There are no courses for dads, they make the visits really hard and he wasn't allowed to be at the birth, so he never had a proper bond with Max. We were both pushed to the limit. We split up when my dad bought us tickets for a holiday to Israel but Carl got arrested. We had to cancel the trip. That was when I realised I couldn't live that kind of life and decided to end the relationship.

Carl is now with many different women, some of whom have children, and he doesn't visit Max much at all. He doesn't take any responsibility for Max's happiness. I can see that he loves his baby deep down, but it's confusing for Max to see him off and on. I'm going to give him an ultimatum: either he sorts out a routine for visiting Max, or he doesn't have any contact at all. I think a clean break would be better in the long run.

Getting a nursery place for Max has been difficult, because I was over 16 and not in full-time education. Eventually my health visitor got one for me, which was great. I can really sort myself out now, make positive plans. I want to go to college to get a nursing qualification and then work in schools or be a physiotherapist.

Everyone assumes young relationships won't last because teenagers don't have any commitment. But once I got pregnant, even though it was by mistake, I really tried hard to make it work. It wasn't because of my age that things didn't work out. It was my judgement of Carl that was wrong. Anyone, of any age, can make a mistake with their choice of partner and not see their faults and weaknesses.

I know my friends are all there for me but I felt very alone in the beginning. The main problem with being a young mum is everyone's attitude. I feel like people treat me differently sometimes. For example, the security guard followed me around a shop one day, assuming I was a thief, because Max was dressed nicely. He wouldn't have done that to a 30-year-old woman whose child was dressed in good clothes.

My own attitude is also a problem sometimes. If I was older I would have more patience with Max. I feel bad for him, not being able to give him everything financially and I miss my freedom a lot and get quite depressed sometimes. It's hard not to take it out on Max. Also I get depressed when I'm out and I see other young girls, because I look flabby and have stretch marks from being pregnant.

The good things about being a young mum are that I will grow up with Max and hopefully be more on his level and understand things better. When he is grown up I will still be young and have time to have a career.

My hopes for the future are to find a career that I enjoy, be able to live comfortably, and know that Max and I will never want for anything.

Mya Elmahelm

No Regrets

I am 16 years old. Last year I had a baby boy who I named Liam. He was born on 4 March.

I met my boyfriend, Oliver, through a friend of mine. We'd gone out for about a year. He was 15 and I was 16. Our relationship was new and we both wanted to have sex. I trusted him and thought it would be a long-term relationship. I used contraception the first time I had sex, but not after that. We didn't like condoms. I just thought it wouldn't happen to me.

When I started to feel sick my friend told my mum and we went to see the doctor together. I thought I was about three months pregnant and I'd spent the whole of that time really worrying, hoping I wasn't. The doctor did a pregnancy test, which turned out positive. I kept thinking, Oh my God.

My mum was upset because it was such a shock. She

was also upset that I didn't tell her myself. This would be her first grandchild. My boyfriend was over the moon but I split up with him when I was about six months pregnant because he was seeing other girls behind my back.

There was never any doubt that I would keep the baby. I don't agree with abortion, although I know for others that it's their choice. When I told people about being pregnant I found out who my friends were. Most people have supported me, but one of them said she didn't want to hang about with me with a baby. My dad just laughed and said he knew this would happen. My mum had just had a baby boy and she said our babies would be like brothers.

I went into hospital on the first Monday in March and Liam was born on the Wednesday. I was crying at the birth. My mum told me she wouldn't lie – it would be agony. The doctor had been really nice to me when I went for my check-ups, but at the delivery the midwife made me feel I was too young, at 15, and as if I was being lazy by asking for an epidural really early on. I had an epidural quite late on in the end. My mum and Oliver's mum were both at the birth and my mum cut the baby's cord. It was an okay experience.

After the birth I felt really happy, although I cried a lot. I only stayed in hospital for one night as I wanted to go home so much. Everyone looked after me when I got home. I didn't feel tired but I felt very emotional for about two months and cried all the time.

Liam looks just like his dad with his hair and eyes. After his birth Oliver came over and we got back together again. He brought chocolates and a card for me. I got on quite well with him for a while. He spent a year in a young offenders' institution and I went to see him there. He loved being a dad. He hated changing dirty nappies, though.

I've since broken up with Oliver as he started threatening me when he got out. I didn't see any future in it so I decided to end it. I feel much better without him. I still want him to see Liam, though, so the courts are arranging access.

Liam is a good baby. He slept straight through for 10 days after the birth. I shared my bedroom with him. At first I found it hard to wake up when he cried, and my mum would get up for him. I didn't find it hard to adjust, though, and soon started getting up for him really easily.

I now wish I hadn't had a baby so young, as I would have liked to go back to my studies. If I could replay my life I would have waited until I was older. I certainly don't want to have another baby until I'm in my 20s. People look at me in the street because I look so young. My health visitor and doctor have been really nice to me, though. The main problem was that at 15 you don't get any state benefits. I just got £20 a week child benefit for the baby.

It was crowded when we all lived at home together but I helped my mum with my brother, who was 14 months, and sister, who was 4. I also got a lot of help back from my mum and dad. I moved into a special housing project for young mothers when Liam was nine months old and I'm about to move into a private flat soon, which I'm looking forward to. Once I've sorted out my flat and got used to being with Liam I can start looking at going back to college.

The good thing about being a teenage mum is the joy I get from my baby. When he wakes up in the morning it's lovely. I really care for him. I feel I have grown up. I'm only 16 but he makes me feel about 20. I feel I'm as good as any other mum, whatever her age.

Andrea Gardiner

I Proved Them Wrong

I conceived on the night of my 15th birthday. My pal and I got more drunk than usual because it was my birthday and we met up with two boys we knew. They weren't drinking because one of them was driving and by the end of the night we ended up going off in their car with them. We knew what was going to happen as soon as we left with them. The lad I was with wasn't the first person I'd slept with, so it wasn't special or anything, it was just a one-night stand.

It was about two months later that I started to have an idea that I was pregnant. I just put it to the back of my mind. I started to get pains in my chest and acid in the back of my throat, but I didn't know what it was. My mum told me it was heartburn. When I mentioned to my pals that I had heartburn, one of them told me that her sister used to get heartburn when she was pregnant. I kind of knew then that I was pregnant.

A month later my mum was told by a psychic that she was going to be a granny. She played a tape of what the psychic had said to me and my best mate. When that bit came on, we just sort of looked at one another.

A month later I knew I was pregnant without a doubt. By this stage I was at least four months gone. I used to lie on my bed every night with a glass of milk and a packet of Rennies and feel the baby kicking. I didn't want an abortion so I didn't tell my mum or anyone else in case they told her – not even a doctor. The only person I told was my best mate, but even then I didn't discuss it with her properly until I was about six months pregnant.

Time went on and nobody even noticed. One day I looked in the mirror and discovered that I was really quite big. I was a bit overweight before getting pregnant so I guess everyone just thought I was putting on weight. I used to wear baggy trousers with a baggy shirt over them to school, so it was difficult to tell, anyway. Sometimes when I lay on the settee in the living room with a cushion on my stomach, the cushion would move if the baby was turning around in my stomach. I'd have to get up in case anyone noticed. The only time my mum noticed I was putting on weight was when I was about seven months pregnant. She prodded my stomach, said 'you're putting on weight' and then walked off. The only time I felt like telling her was about a month before, when I was six months gone, and we moved to a pub. I got told to carry all the heavy boxes up to the new flat and my back was aching. But I didn't tell her.

About two weeks later I finally went to see a doctor. She was really good with me and told me that I'd need to tell my mum, because she'd have to send a midwife to my house to see that my baby and I were okay. She then checked my baby's heartbeat to make sure everything was all right. She told me to make an appointment to see her with my mum in two days' time.

I discussed with my pal how I was going to tell my mum and decided to write her a letter. I left it on her bed so that she would read it just before going to sleep and have time for it to sink in. I had a maths exam in the morning and my doctor's appointment in the afternoon. Unfortunately things didn't go to plan because my mum didn't read the letter until the next morning. When I woke up the whole house was in uproar, which didn't give me a good start to my exam. After a big argument I got sent to school and told we'd discuss it when I got home. I had to run out of the exam hall that morning to be sick. I think it was more to do with worry about going home and facing the music, as I hadn't ever had morning sickness before.

When I got home my mum and I went to the doctor's. My mum said I should give the baby up for adoption and we ended up arguing and both left in tears. That was only the beginning. My mum, her boyfriend and my oldest sister all started going on at me, telling me that I would never cope if I kept the baby, that they wouldn't help me, that I'd never go out or get a boyfriend; basically, that I was too young and would never have a life. My other sister insisted on me keeping the baby, but she was only saying that to get at my mum, as they'd fallen out. The only person whose advice I truly appreciated was my dad's. He told me to do what I felt was best.

My mum got a social worker to try to tell me what to

do. They all ganged up on me and would have me in tears for hours, right up to the birth. The social worker was a right bitch and told me I couldn't cope and that I was really immature, sitting there crying and not telling anyone that I was pregnant until now. I wonder why?! I stuck to my guns and told them I was keeping my baby. No one really spoke to me much after that, apart from my sisters and dad, until I had the baby. I think my mum was hoping that I would change my mind.

I woke up one morning with uncomfortable twinges, and after breakfast, as the pains weren't going away, we made our way over to the hospital. I started having gas and air as by now the contractions were getting worse. The nurse broke my waters to speed things up. Eventually I was screaming so much from the pain I ended up having a pethridine jab and four epidurals. I don't know which was worse, being in labour or the huge needles in my spine. I was violently sick because of all the gas and air and had to have more drugs because the epidurals had slowed down the contractions. Then the baby started losing oxygen because of all the drugs. I finally gave birth to a baby girl but she had to be immediately taken away because she had breathing difficulties. I had been in labour for 22 hours, but it felt like longer. Then I haemorrhaged and later fell asleep.

When I woke up in the maternity ward there was a photo of my baby next to my bed. One of the nurses came over and told me she was okay. I went down to see her. She was with lots of premature babies and the nurse there was quite protective of her; I don't think she was trying to be nasty, but she made me feel uneasy.

I took to motherhood quite well. It all just clicked into

place. The nurses tried to show me what to do and how to do it. I don't know why but it felt like I already knew. People started to visit and I got loads of cards and gifts – more than I thought I would. I stayed in hospital for five days, which felt like a lifetime, then was allowed home after persuading the nurses that I would be able to take care of my baby without their help.

Once I got home, I found motherhood much harder work. There were bottles to wash and make up, clothes to wash, nappies to change, housework, plus looking after my baby. It may not sound like a lot, but it's very tiring. I suppose I was quite lucky because she was sleeping right through the night after about two weeks, I know most babies aren't the same.

My friends have been great. They don't treat me any differently. Other people reacted more when the baby was first born because I was only 15. I live in a small town and everyone knew my mum because she ran a pub. They all thought it was scandalous that I was having a baby and called me a slag; but they're just small-minded people in a small town. They all thought I wouldn't be able to cope, but I proved everyone wrong, so they don't really say anything to me now.

When my baby was about six months old I got a flat from the council. I was 16 and just glad that I was getting a place of my own. After being there for a couple of months fungi started to appear through the floor and walls because of damp, so two days before Christmas I was moved into a new flat. It was all a big rush as the flat needed decorating and carpets putting down.

I have never had any major problems with my baby; even when she was teething she was good. But as soon as she hit two, it was like she turned into a monster. The tantrums came as soon as she didn't get her own way, and she would bite, scratch, kick and bang her head on the floor. When she starts she gets put in her room, which works better than smacking her, and it gives her a chance to calm down.

My wee girl doesn't have much to do with her dad. She usually stays with him on Friday night but is back home by 12 o'clock the next day and doesn't really spend that much time with him on her own.

I have recently got engaged to my boyfriend. We've been together for two years and my wee girl has known him since she was six months old, so she can't really remember him not being there. They get on brilliantly together; he's more of a dad to her than her real dad. He sees her every day, plays with her, has tea with her, puts her to bed and is basically there for her.

I've now got a five-month-old baby with my boyfriend, which we're really happy about, although it wasn't planned. I'd always said that I would never have another baby and that I was going to go out and enjoy myself, but I've been out and done everything, really. Ever since my wee girl was six months old I've been going out, having a drink, etc., at least once a week. I'm in a steady relationship and now I've been offered a house with a garden, so it means my kids can get out in the summer and not be stuck in a flat with a busy road outside.

The good thing about being a young mum is that I'll be able to relate to my kids more easily when they're teenagers and I won't have nappies to change or bottles to wash when I'm in my 30s – hopefully! I've got an interview at the local college for a course on childcare and education, which I hope will lead to a job in a nursery or perhaps social work. My boyfriend will look after the children when I'm at college.

Things have worked out well for me, but everyone's different. My advice to any young teenager planning on having a baby is to wait. It won't do you any harm. If you're going out with someone and they love you, then they'll wait. You should go and get a career, make sure you're in a steady, *happy* relationship and then, if it's what you both want, go for it. But remember it's an expensive and tiring business. If, like me, it's an accident, then do what your heart tells you. If you are headstrong and independent, you can do it. If you choose an abortion, choose it because you want it, not because your family or boyfriend want it. Otherwise you might hate yourself for ever. The same goes with adoption; you might hate yourself for giving her away. On the other hand, if you keep your baby then you might end up resenting it if you didn't really want it.

Do what you want to do because, at the end of the day, you're the one who has to live with the decision. Whatever your choice, make sure it's the right one, and hopefully things will work out for you.

Helen Tomlinson

Just My Luck

Right from the start I knew I was pregnant; although I didn't really believe it could happen to me. I didn't look pregnant, I didn't feel pregnant. My boyfriend and I used condoms, but they kept splitting. No problem, I thought, just take the morning-after pill. My mate takes it all the time. But I was one of the unlucky ones because it made me very sick. I didn't know I should have taken another dose as it never had a chance to work. Soon I just knew I was pregnant. My breasts were sore and I felt sick. It would be just my luck.

I knew I had to get it sorted out quickly. I had a pregnancy test at Brook. It came out positive. I was eight weeks already. Why me? I thought. I was upset and angry. I was 17 and my boyfriend was 16. It was a nice idea having a baby, but I just couldn't. A 16-year-old lad is quite immature really, neither of us had a job or any money, and our relationship wasn't really going anywhere.

My boyfriend didn't react much at first when I told him. Then it went to his head a bit. He kept on saying he'd tell my nan (I live with her) and we could get a flat. Sure, I thought, in about 10 years' time! I couldn't tell my nan. Who knows what the shock would have done to her?

Suddenly there were all these things to do. First I got a referral from my GP for the abortion, plus a talk about going on the pill afterwards. Of course I'm going on the bloody pill afterwards, I thought. My nan knew all the staff at the surgery and I was terrified someone would tell her. I asked the receptionists not to say anything. Everything you tell a doctor is confidential, of course, but I was positive my nan would find out somehow and I ended up in tears.

Then I had an examination, and they arranged for a date for the abortion. My friends came with me. To be honest, I felt a bit selfish. I was scared of having an operation, not of losing my baby.

I told my nan I was going to Stratford-upon-Avon for the day. Looking back, it only really hit me what I was doing when I got there. People were so normal. My friends had to leave me and go and stay in the waiting room. I felt so alone. I've never cried so much in all my life; all these bottled-up tears suddenly let loose. But when I found out there was one girl who was 16 in the room and 12 weeks gone, I didn't feel as lonely.

About 20 minutes later a girl was wheeled in from her operation. She looked groggy. Then it hit me. OH GOD, I'M NEXT! I was hysterical. I was too scared to get on the operating table, and at first they couldn't inject me because I was in such a state. All I remember next is coming round and feeling sick. It was over. I felt my stomach. A couple of hours ago I was pregnant and now I wasn't. I couldn't get my head around it. The surgeon told me the operation had gone well and gave me a leaflet on dos and don'ts for the next couple of days. I met my friends in the waiting room. They couldn't believe I'd had an operation, it was all over so quickly. Then all the girls who'd had abortions helped themselves to tea and sandwiches. It was weird.

I told my boyfriend all about it the next day. I was worried that he'd go off me, as I couldn't have sex for about three weeks, but he was really sweet. I had a bit of tummy ache when I got home. I just couldn't believe I'd got away with it without my nan finding out.

Looking back, it was the best thing to do. It was the only decision to make at the time. For one thing, my boyfriend and I have split up once or twice since. I would have been on my own with a baby if I hadn't had the abortion. I read stories in magazines about girls who really regret having an abortion and I wonder why I don't. But lately my boyfriend has started thinking more and more about it and sometimes he says he wishes we could have had the baby.

Everything's fine now, though. We're engaged, and his mum and dad know about the abortion. They were shocked but agreed that it was the best thing to do. I'm just pleased it didn't ruin everything. We're living together now and both working. We do want a baby but not yet. At least I know I'm capable of getting pregnant – it's a great feeling.

Kim Black

I've Kept My Promise

People said that I was in denial but I always knew I was pregnant – I just couldn't tell anyone. Everybody saw me as the person who did everything right and never did anything wrong. I thought that if I told anybody they would push me out of their lives or be nasty to me. I also thought that if they found out, they would make me have an abortion and I knew with all my heart I couldn't do that.

When my periods stopped I knew I was pregnant and so I never did a pregnancy test. I kept telling myself I would go to the doctor's and then I would tell everyone. But I never plucked up the courage to make the appointment. One day I sat with the phone in one hand and the doctor's number in the other. I dialled the numbers but the line was engaged. I wasn't ever able to dial the number again. From that day it felt like a dream and one day I would wake up...

When I was alone, I would be in tears. I would promise myself that whatever happened the baby would have a good life and I would do anything for the baby. I feel that despite what has happened I have kept my promise. Most of the time I felt love towards the baby, but a few times it felt as if I had an alien inside me and I just wished it would go away as it was changing my life and I didn't like it. I wanted it to be how it was before.

During my pregnancy I exercised, carried heavy things about and even had a minor operation on my leg. Every time I did something like that I would feel so guilty but if I didn't carry on as normal, then somebody would want to know why. That was a question I just couldn't answer. I don't smoke or drink so I never hurt the baby in that way. Christmas was a hard time. I had to pretend everything was fine and that I had no worries, but in reality I had no idea what the year ahead would bring.

I started putting on weight and at first nobody noticed, as I wore baggy clothes anyway. For the first time in my life I found myself spending ages trying on clothes, finding out which ones hid my bump, which was growing bigger and bigger by the day. I also learnt how to position myself so that I didn't look pregnant.

My mum started asking questions when I was about six months gone, but I just denied it. I didn't even know how pregnant I was. At the time, keeping the secret to myself seemed the best option but, looking back, it was something I shouldn't have done. I wouldn't want anybody to go through it, as you're watching yourself and others all the time. Now, if I could replay everything, I would definitely tell someone.

Then one day in town my mum asked me for the final

time if I was pregnant. I will never forget the look on her face as I admitted it to her. I can't really describe it. She didn't seem angry, just completely shocked. From that moment she has been the greatest and has never questioned why I didn't say anything before.

That day I went to the doctor's. They thought I was about seven months pregnant and that I was having twins. A few days later I was told I was eight months pregnant and only having one baby. Everybody that dealt with me was really good. The only thing they were shocked about was that I was eight months pregnant and had managed to keep it a secret.

A social worker came to visit me a few days later. I had already said before she came to see me that I felt it was best for me and the baby if it was adopted. I have to admit that I thought this would be the easy option, but I found out it is the hardest thing you can do. I thought at the time that I was too young, living at home with no job and no money. I couldn't have given the baby the good life she deserved. My mum and the social worker listened and didn't put me under any pressure. It was entirely my decision. My thoughts changed day by day, but I finally made the decision and settled with it. It was best for the baby.

I went into labour 10 days after my mum and dad found out. It went really well and I didn't even need any pain relief. When my daughter was born I was very confused. I loved her to bits but I knew adoption was the right thing to do. I spent the whole morning in the hospital room by myself, crying. I asked for her to be put in the nursery. I was scared I'd get too attached to her. I left the hospital that afternoon and she stayed there. The midwife took photos of her and me together for us.

My daughter was in hospital for seven days. I visited her every day and took photos and my family came to visit. I then took her to the foster parents' house, where she stayed for four months because I changed my mind several times and it took a while to make all the arrangements with her adoptive parents. I visited twice a week. I would bath her, feed her, change her and take her for walks. My social worker advised me that it would be best for both of us if I stopped seeing her when she was three months old. During this time all I could think about was what I would do when I had to say goodbye to her. I will never forget that day as long as I live. I felt a total emptiness. The future was suddenly a complete vacuum. Even though I chose the parents for my daughter, which made it a bit easier, I had no idea where she would be, what her life would be like, or even whether I would see her again. She went to live with her adoptive parents four weeks later.

I think of my daughter all the time and I miss her so much. I have contact once a year through letters. She is with her new parents who love her just as much and respect the fact that she is my daughter too. But I hope she doesn't hate me for what I have done.

Debbie Curran

It Takes Two

It was January four years ago when I first met Dave. He was 14 years old and I had just turned 15. I thought he was nice looking and really funny, but I didn't fancy him and soon forgot about him as he didn't go to our school. It was over three months before I saw him again. I was out with my mates, just doing the usual – smoking and getting drunk – when he arrived with his friend. We got talking; he was really good to get on with. After a while the crowd filtered out. It was about 10 o'clock and I had long since polished off a bottle of Thunderbird, so I was feeling kind of drunk. Dave leaned over and kissed me and I kissed him back. That night I ended up giving him a blow-job. I only told my closest friends and promised myself I would never do it again – I felt terrible.

Then Dave moved to my school. We never spoke about what had happened and soon I found a new love interest: Joe. We saw each other for about a week, but then he went back with his ex. I was heartbroken. I really loved him – at least, I thought I did.

I decided to move on and forget about Joe. I spent one night with a lad called Martin, who I'd liked for a while, and a month later I slept with a soldier. Reading this you might think I was a slag, but I wasn't – I was just very naïve (and also a bit drunk).

When I went back to school after the holidays I realised just how much I still liked Joe. I decided to make him jealous and so I met up with Dave again in the local park. It started to rain so we headed for the bushes. We sat talking for ages. He told me he really liked me and started to kiss me. I didn't try to stop him. We ended up having sex that night. The next week at school I couldn't face him; what if he'd only done it because he'd been drinking? I felt so stupid. Eventually he caught up with me. He said he was sorry for taking advantage of me and that he wanted us to stay friends. I thought that was so sweet. A week later I made my friend phone him and ask him if he'd go out with me. He said yes. That night he phoned me and we talked for over two hours. He invited me to his house the next day. We had a great day together; his mum and dad were out all day and we had sex twice.

That night, though, I heard a few rumours that he'd been mouthing off about what had happened and the next day I heard that he'd tried to shag some other girl. Despite this I carried on seeing him until he dumped me. I was a bit pissed off until Joe started to show some interest in me again. I'd made him jealous without even realising! Three days after my 16th birthday Joe and I had sex. I was in heaven – until the next day, when he decided it had been a mistake and didn't want to go out with me.

I was devastated. One of his friends wrote 'slag' all over one of my school books and Joe told everyone I'd been calling him on the phone and then hanging up. How could I explain to him that I'd been trying to tell him I thought I was two months pregnant?

It was November and we were doing our mock GCSEs. I went to the doctor's for a pregnancy test and got the results a few days later in my dinner break, between two exams. I was really calm at first – my two friends were more upset than I was. I sat on the park bench, just staring into space. My mind was completely numb. Another of my mates came over to ask what was wrong and I just collapsed in tears. At the same time Joe walked past and overheard one of my friends say, 'She's pregnant.' Joe went white with shock. I don't know how I managed to sit through my exam that afternoon. I could feel everyone watching me and I knew that no one was really concentrating on the test.

According to the doctor I got pregnant around the last week of September. I'd had sex with Dave the week before fertilisation and with Joe the week after. The baby was probably Dave's, according to calculations, but I couldn't be 100 per cent sure. Joe and I weren't speaking, so it was Dave that I turned to.

At first Dave was really great, saying he'd support me, but I knew he really wanted me to have an abortion. At the antenatal clinic at hospital, where the doctor had arranged an appointment for me, there were baby pictures everywhere. The nurse was very clinical and booked me in for an abortion for the next Monday. I went home and told my friends that there was something wrong with the baby and that if I didn't have an abortion I'd miscarry and possibly ruin my chances of ever having children.

I waited for Dave to turn up that night. He never did. On Sunday night I went out as usual and had to cope with Joe staring at me all night. I wanted to talk to him but I didn't know what to say.

The next day I phoned up the hospital and cancelled my appointment for the abortion. I knew I had to tell my parents. That evening at home I was really quiet and when my dad asked what was wrong, I just broke down and said, 'I can't tell you, you'll go mad.' I think he guessed; when I finally blurted out that I was pregnant, my dad closed his eyes and my mum walked out. I kept saying, 'I don't want it, I don't want it.'

The next morning was awful. You could have cut the atmosphere with a knife. I went to school without saying a word to Mum and Dad. That night, however, we had a talk and I decided that I was going to keep my baby. I gave up smoking and drinking and started getting morning sickness straight away.

I felt really uncomfortable talking about the pregnancy – even to my parents. It just felt weird. I had to tell my cousin, as she had seen me at the antenatal clinic. I also told my grandparents, but not my other grandma, as her mother had just died and I didn't want to make her feel worse. My teachers at school were really great and gave me extra help when I needed it, but I still noticed people staring and whispering about me.

Dave and I had a lot of rows while I was pregnant. He yelled at me because I'd taken drugs before and I began to resent him. I'd ignore him at school or just smile quickly and keep walking. I blamed him for the pregnancy. He was still going with other girls while I was expecting his baby. It made me feel angry but also worthless, and I hated him for it.

I left school for good when I was seven months pregnant. I went to Malta for a two-week holiday but had a terrible time – I couldn't sunbathe, I didn't want to go swimming and I felt tired all the time.

Leaving school was awful. I was really lonely and miserable. My friends rang and came round but it wasn't the same. I became very depressed and was admitted to hospital for a week, suffering from hypertension. I just lay in bed, crying all the time. I was supposed to rest so all I did was eat and sleep. In one week I put on a stone.

While in hospital I went into labour, a month early. I cried and cried, I was so scared. I wanted my mum. She came as soon as she could. I just kept saying, 'I don't want a baby, take it back!' At 10.25 a.m., 18 May, William was born. I held him in my arms and looked at him. I just couldn't believe it. I was 16 years old and I had a baby.

I slept all day and all night after the birth. The nurses looked after the baby. We stayed in hospital for two weeks, as William was premature and had to be tube-fed and sleep in an incubator. It was really boring and lonely in hospital and I became very depressed. Dave and his parents came to see me, even though I didn't really want them to. He brought a teddy and a card, but I was so angry that I ripped the card up a few days later.

Two days after getting out of hospital I sat my GCSEs. God only knows how I managed to pass with Bs and Cs, as I didn't do any revision.

I saw Dave one night when I was out and we had a massive row. He started crying and telling me how his mum said he should have a blood test, but that he believed William was his. I told Dave he couldn't see William and I wanted nothing to do with him. I know it sounds heartless but I turned away and left him crying. I was so confused and angry and I suppose I took my anger out on him. It wasn't right that I, a 16-year-old, should have to have a baby. I know it sounds like a cliché, but I always thought it would never happen to me. I was smart, pretty and popular. I blamed Dave for ruining my life. After the exams he moved to another town and I never saw him again. Now I wish I hadn't been so cruel.

As well as going to college now, I also work at night to support William. The Child Support Agency has done little to make Dave do his bit. They say he denies being William's dad, which hurts me. I never wanted Dave's money, I just wanted him to be there for me. I wanted him to realise I needed him and his support. I sometimes wish Dave would get in touch. I don't want William to miss out by not having a dad.

Even though I go out with my new friends I still feel that I miss out. I don't think that I'm a slag – just unfortunate. I know girls who sleep with a different lad every week and never get pregnant. It just seems so unfair. I have never regretted my decision to keep the baby but I do regret getting pregnant so young. Being pregnant was the worst time of my life. I have never felt so low and I don't know how I coped alone – I only just did. I could never go through all that again. Now I am much more careful about relationships. I realise just how dangerous sex can be.

I still feel lonely, but for now it's just the two of us. Who knows, some day William could have a new dad, and we'll be one happy family.

Mandy Taylor

Truly, Madly, Deeply

I was 15 and thought no one could be as special as Mike. I truly believed we would be together for the rest of our lives, like many first loves. Mike was 21 and had his own place, so privacy was never a problem. We started a sexual relationship and didn't always use protection. Week after week would go by and things were great.

Then after two months of no periods, I began to suspect something was wrong. I mentioned it to friends but decided to leave things a little longer. Another month passed and eventually one of my friends told me I had to do something. So after school my friends and I went to our local family planning centre. They confirmed what I'd chosen to ignore. I was pregnant. I then had a scan and discovered I was three and a half months. I've never felt so scared and numb in all my life. I was given advice but it drifted in one ear and out the other. All I could think about was how to tell my mum.

I chose not to. Things were very difficult at home as it was. This would have been the last thing to discuss around the dinner table. Telling Mike was no problem. He didn't say a lot or show much emotion. I then found out he had another girlfriend and we split up. Now I really was on my own – scared, lonely, hurt and, most of all, pregnant.

The weeks went by as I tried to get over Mike. I threw myself back into school work and again pushed things to one side. I was hiding things quite well, considering. But soon I ran out of excuses to get off PE. Then one day the tears came and my PE teacher soon realised the problem. She was great and didn't tell me off. She had just had a baby herself and told me about all the joys of parenthood. I was then sent to my headmistress, who gave me three days to tell my mum.

On the very last evening I told her. I asked her not to make me have the baby, but I only said that to make her not so angry at me. It wasn't what I really wanted. I wanted that baby more than you could ever imagine. To make things worse I felt my baby's first foetal movements that night.

Mum wasn't angry; she was more disappointed, as any mother probably would be. After a week of not speaking or making eye contact, she and her boyfriend decided there wasn't enough room or money for a baby. This hurt me, not only because I was going to lose my baby, but also because my welfare was not their concern. I cried and cried until I was ill. I begged and pleaded with them to change their minds but with no success.

By now I was 20 weeks, or 5 months, pregnant. I prayed that it was too late for anything to be done. To my dismay there were two places that did terminations so late on. Mum didn't hesitate to book me in. The week before the termination was the worst ever. The pain and hurt was so severe it felt like I had been split in two. Not even the longest, sharpest knife could produce that pain. Something left my soul that week.

We arrived at the clinic for the termination and I was given some counselling, but it didn't make it any easier. I was then told what to expect the next day. I wasn't scared; the feeling of loss was too deep for that. I wasn't allowed to eat or drink anything and was given a drip with glucose in it for energy. A doctor inserted a needle into my stomach below my tummy button to remove the fluid around the baby's head. This was what killed my baby. I was then alone. I felt so lonely and very upset, praying to God that maybe the needle hadn't worked. I waited to feel my baby move, but nothing came. Then my drip was changed and another one was fitted with some liquid in it that induced labour. This took many hours and I had to have pethidine to reduce the pain of the contractions. Then my waters were broken. Many hours later I gave birth to a little boy. He wasn't alive. I was left alone again and cried myself to sleep. Much later, after having a D/C under general anaesthetic to remove all last traces of the pregnancy in the womb, I was reunited with Mum. Somehow, even having my own mum there didn't comfort me in any way. I was checked over and then allowed home.

Days, weeks and months went by and still each day I'd cry for my loss. I didn't feel any shame over my grieving. I had counselling but nothing put back what I'd lost. I carried on through school, then left home and went to college. I still thought about my baby boy every day.

I am now 20. Six months ago I gave birth to a baby girl after a long seven-day labour. Kira is the best thing that has ever happened to me. 'Truly magnificent' isn't strong enough to describe how I felt when I held her in my arms for the first time.

The birth also brought back a lot of memories of my first baby, but most of all, the feeling of loss. I had postnatal depression and started seeing a counsellor, who suggested I name my first baby and put his name in the book of remembrance at the hospital chapel. I've been carrying this loss for five years now, and now that my new baby is here, it's time to lay him to rest. It doesn't mean I've forgotten him; I have given him his own special place that I can always visit.

At 20, with a wonderful partner in my own house and with a secure income, all I can say is that it is hard enough to raise a baby. At 15 I couldn't have managed, either financially or emotionally. It was my mother who made the decision for me to have an abortion. I can't begin to imagine how hard that must have been and I can now see why she made it. Even if we make the right decisions in life, it doesn't mean that no one is going to get hurt. Sometimes there isn't a right decision, just two hard choices.

Tanya Jones

Out of Time

Before I got pregnant I was a bubbly and outgoing person. I was 19, at college, and enjoyed a very active social life. I used to go clubbing or just hang out with my friends – all the things you'd do at my age. I didn't have any plans for the future academically, although I was planning to go to Camp America the following year.

When I found out that I was pregnant I was devastated. I knew there might have been a possibility because I'd had unprotected sex. Because of various reasons I ran out of time to get the morning-after pill. I didn't know about the IUD, which also works as another form of emergency contraception if you have it fitted within five days of unprotected sex. I hoped and prayed, but I didn't really think it would happen to me.

When my period was late I took a home pregnancy test. Although it seemed positive, it wasn't very clear and

I found it hard to believe. I just carried on with my day-to-day life as normal. Over the next month I started feeling sick. I also felt really tired and tearful, and my belly started to feel tight. So I decided to go to Brook to get another test done. That also came up positive.

I felt like my life had collapsed. I suddenly felt as if I wasn't myself any more. I knew now that my freedom had gone. I wasn't sure how I was going to cope. I wasn't even responsible for myself, much less someone else.

When I told my mum she didn't speak to me for a week. She said I had let her down and she felt ashamed and embarrassed. When she did finally speak to me she called me a lot of horrible names. My boyfriend wasn't very supportive at first. He was more interested in his own life and how the baby was going to affect him. I could never have aborted the baby. I felt that it was my own fault and I just had to deal with it. I managed to block it out of my head for the next three months.

During the pregnancy I felt very distressed. I felt alone: I had no one to talk to and I had all these fears in my head. I didn't know whether I was coming or going. It seemed as though everyone was talking about me and looking down on me because of my age. I felt really embarrassed and tried to cover up that I was pregnant. I was also very tired and run down because of the work-load at college and trying to maintain my part-time job.

However, towards the end of my pregnancy when I'd finished college and left work, I felt a lot more relaxed and started to look forward to my parentcraft classes. By this time my mum started to accept the situation, so I could discuss it openly with her and ask her questions. My boyfriend's views also changed and he gave me a lot of emotional support.

My life now is all about my son. Now that I have Morgan my way of thinking has completely changed: everything I do, I have to think of my son first. I still do part-time work but most of the time I just take care of Morgan. My partner works and goes to college so he isn't around much to help. Having a baby means there is less time for one another and that is a strain, but he has given me enough support so that I can be pretty independent of my mum. She has been involved, but has two young children herself, so her time is limited. I was placed in a hostel for a while but I have my own place now and feel more settled. Hopefully my boyfriend will live with me permanently.

Life is a bit more of a struggle physically and financially. My friends don't seem to include me any more when they go out, and that gets me down. I find it easier to get on with people who have children these days, but don't find it easy to meet other mums – so life can seem a bit dull. Instead of going to Camp America I stayed on at college to finish my GNVQ. But now I want to go to university to do a degree. Not just for myself, but also as an example to my son. So having Morgan has given me plans for the future which I wasn't focusing on before.

Rosy Cooper

The Easy Way Out?

I got pregnant when I was 15 years old. I'd been seeing Pete, who was 16, for 7 months. Pete was the only person I told; I didn't even tell a doctor. His initial reaction was fear, but then he started using 'our secret' as a way of controlling me for the next five months. One night after he threatened to kill himself and then hit me several times, I ended the relationship. He said he'd tell my parents that I was pregnant, but I lied and told him I'd had my period. He believed me and left me alone.

The day before I was due to start my final year at school I told my best friend, Cath, that I thought I was about six months pregnant and had finally booked a doctor's appointment the next day. We told a third friend, Karen, and all skipped school to go. At the doctor's I was told it was essential I went straight to the hospital for an ultrasound. We sent Karen back to school to cover for us.

Still in my school uniform, I was then examined by a doctor, who told me that people shouldn't have sex before marriage. Until this point I had been very calm and collected, but this remark opened the floodgates. For some reason, then unbeknown to me, I was sent for a second scan.

Then my aunt turned up. She was a teacher at my school and, suspecting I was pregnant for some time, had pressured Karen into telling her where I was. She drove us home and I told my parents.

My mum's initial reaction was anger and my dad's sympathy. I sat on the couch and my dad put his arms around me while my mum rampaged up and down the room. That night I went to tell Pete that I was still pregnant with his child and that my parents wouldn't allow any contact between us or between him and the baby.

A week later we learnt that a bubble had been detected on the baby's brain during a scan and that this might lead to brain damage. I was forced to leave school but fully intended to return. I carried on studying at home with work sent via my aunt.

The birth was quite difficult and lasted 36 hours. After much confusion with a midwife who refused to believe that my waters had broken, I gave birth to Alexandra on 28 December at 2.53 p.m. She weighed 7 pounds and 10 ounces.

When Alexandra was a week old we had to take her for a brain scan. My most vivid memory is of her screaming as they tried to insert a tube into her hand, into which ink would be injected to see her brain more clearly. After trying for an hour they gave up, as her veins were too small. Later we were given the news: her brain wasn't properly formed.

They couldn't tell us at this stage how she would be affected or how severe her disabilities might be.

My mum was now really supportive. I stayed at home with Alexandra until she was three months old and then, with the help of my mother and a childminder, I returned to school for my final year.

I had a real fight to go back to school. An average of six girls a year at my school fall pregnant and are excluded, which I think is appalling. Because my aunt fought on my behalf they eventually allowed me back. I was the only one in the school's history to return and complete my education. Since then, only one other girl has been allowed back so it doesn't seem as if things are changing.

This was my most difficult time. All my friends had started to become involved with the rave scene and I was unable to go because of Alexandra and the amount of school work I had to catch up on. I'd missed six months. Eventually I sat my GCSEs and passed all eight. To say I was pleased was an understatement.

During the summer we realised that Alexandra wasn't developing properly. When she was one, we were told that she should start physiotherapy and hydrotherapy to reduce the stiffness in her limbs. When she was two, we were told for certain that she suffered from spastic cerebral palsy, which affected all her muscles. Alexandra continued to go to the childminder and I carried on studying for my A levels. There was no school near by that met her needs so we had to fight to get her into a special school in the next town.

When Alexandra was 3 and I was 18, I decided to go to Liverpool to do a degree at university, returning home every weekend and in the holidays. Alexandra lived with Mum and Dad. I graduated with a 2.1 and with the support of my family went to America for four months. I worked on a special-needs camp and did some travelling.

Alexandra lives with my parents and my mother is the main caregiver. She requires a lot of care and will never be independent: she is unable to wash, dress or feed herself, she can't walk and has an electric wheelchair. She still calls me Mum, but we have more of a sibling relationship.

I have just finished a teaching qualification and am planning on taking my master's degree in Canada, where I lived when I was young. Before that, I need two years' teaching experience, so I'm looking for jobs near home. At the moment, everyone realises I can't combine looking after Alexandra with my career but I have an agreement with Mum that I will eventually care for her full-time, as my parents are getting older and it will be too much for them at some point.

I know that there will be a crunch time and it's going to be extremely difficult. I am always concerned about having to care for Alexandra by myself and I worry about my future, especially if it comes to having more children. I worry about whether they will be disabled, whether my partner will accept Alexandra, and whether I will cope. I'm trying to take it all step-by-step.

Pete has only visited Alexandra once, after I pursued a claim for maintenance through the Child Support Agency in order to help secure her future. He hardly spoke a word to her. She sat on my lap and asked him questions such as 'What colour car do you drive?' I naïvely thought that after seeing his daughter, Pete would want to be part of her life, but he doesn't want any more contact with either of us, even though he only lives five minutes away.

I feel very bitter about Pete and his family. Their rejection of Alexandra totally devastated me. My parents have sacrificed so much to give me the life I have. Pete 'sacrifices' £45 a month, which I put into an account for Alexandra's future. I'd rather he sacrificed £45 of his time. Alexandra is worth more than that, and so am I.

I think that any mother feels a loss of identity when a new baby arrives, and this is particularly true of teenage mothers. It is important to develop yourself as well as raising a child. I could not have accomplished what I have done without taking all the help on offer. My parents have been brilliant. They gave me the opportunity to grow and I am now hopefully embarking on a successful teaching career. Education is extremely important, but unfortunately so many teenage mothers give up school.

Having a baby isn't the easy way out. I have struggled and suffered, but I have been successful despite the odds being stacked against me. I believe that my experience helps prove that teenage pregnancies are not disastrous, and I hope it will encourage other teenage mums to strive towards their own goals.

Dawn Evans

No Turning Back

A few years ago in March I was going out with a boy called Jamie. I was 14 and he was 16. He was my older brother's friend and I'd fancied him for years, so when he asked me out I jumped at the chance. But he was well experienced, unlike me, and to keep him I had to agree to having sex with him.

We split up after a month or so and that was that. I missed a period in August, around five months later, but I couldn't work out why. I hadn't had sex with anyone since Jamie, so I thought I couldn't be pregnant. I confided in my best friend, who said I should take a home pregnancy test just in case. It was positive. I cried and cried, I was so shocked. I just hoped it would all be a mistake. It made me sick thinking about the baby inside me. I hated it. At the time I was a gymnast representing my country. I was making my way in life and this was shattering all my dreams. My friend and I decided I must have got pregnant just fooling around with other lads.

I went to the doctor's and he confirmed that I was pregnant. He suggested I tell my mum immediately. But I couldn't; I thought she'd kill me. No one could tell I was pregnant as I was still very thin, only six and a half stone. But my friend's mum found out and told my mum two weeks later. She cried a lot but she didn't react as badly as I thought she would. She was great.

My mum and I talked about it for ages. I was determined to have an abortion. At the surgery, the doctor gave me a check-up and then looked at me, rather confused. He told me he thought I was at least seven months pregnant and that I needed to have a scan. Apparently some girls can carry on having periods even when they're pregnant. I was in tears, realising that it was too late for an abortion and I would have to have the baby. Sure enough, the scan showed I was six and a half months pregnant. It was Jamie's baby.

I decided adoption would be for the best. Most of my family wanted me to keep the baby but my mum supported me. As the pregnancy progressed more and more people found out. Everybody was really shocked, as I'd imagined, but no one was nasty or horrible to me.

I had no problems with the pregnancy – apart, that is, from growing more and more attached to the baby. I thought adoption would be best but that didn't stop me loving my child. In the end I couldn't go ahead. I knew deep down that when the day came, I wouldn't be able to go through with it. My family were all relieved when I said I wanted to keep the baby. The doctors and hospital staff were fantastic, really nice.

On 30 December I felt pains in my stomach. At 11.30 p.m. I was taken to hospital. The labour was really easy and over quite quickly. My baby girl was born at 2.17 a.m. on New Year's Eve morning, weighing 8 pounds 10½ ounces. I named her Rosa. When I held her for the first time, the feeling of love was indescribable. It was just overwhelming. I'd never felt so much love for one person.

When I brought Rosa home I was really scared but I knew I had 100 per cent support from my family. It was also hard because I had to go back to school. I hated leaving Rosa but I wanted to go back and finish as I had big ambitions. I finished school with all my GCSEs and now I've just finished my A levels.

I have fulfilled all the dreams that I had before having Rosa, but it's been down to determination and support from my family. It's been a long hard slog and I wouldn't advise anyone to have a baby so young.

I'm now living with my boyfriend, Shaun, who I've been with for three years. We both work. Rosa doesn't see her real father, but she doesn't need him. She has everything any little girl could wish for; we are all a family now.

Jessie Matthews

By the Look on Her Face

It was summertime and I had been going out with Simon for about six months. I was 19 and he was my first boyfriend. My periods are normally very regular, so when I was two weeks late I went straight to my local family planning clinic and gave in a urine sample. I thought there would be some other explanation for my late period. But when the nurse came and took me into a private room, I could tell by the look on her face that I was pregnant.

I didn't know how to react. I didn't know if I should cry or be happy. They asked me what I wanted to do. For them it was just like deciding what clothes to wear. I walked out of the clinic hardly aware of where I was going – I wouldn't even have noticed Oasis walking past. It was such a horrible feeling.

I went for a walk to clear my mind and then went

home and phoned my boyfriend and asked him to come over.

He could tell from my face there was something wrong. I told him I was pregnant and asked him what he thought I should do, but he just said it was up to me. He didn't really help me out. I wanted him to tell me it would be all right and cuddle me, but he just went back home. He telephoned me that night but didn't come round.

I thought about it for a week and then built up the courage to tell my parents. I didn't know how they were going to react, but my mum was very good and helped me come to my decision without pushing me at all.

I phoned up the family planning clinic and told them I wanted an abortion. They booked me in for a check-up and then made an appointment for the abortion. I realised this would be when Simon was on holiday with his cousin. I begged him to stay but he refused and that pushed us further apart. He also told his mum about my decision. She is against abortion for religious reasons and she kept phoning me and trying to get me to change my mind. Everyone – except my mum and my best friend, Vicky – started pestering me about it. The one person who I'd thought would look after me, talk to me and just be there for me, was Simon, but the abortion changed things between us and he became very distant. I felt really alone, except for my mum and Vicky. I kept telling myself that I had made the right decision.

I went to the hospital the day after Simon went on holiday. Mum went with me and was there when I came round from the operation that evening. I just wanted Simon to be there. I was given the all-clear and went straight home to bed because I was in such pain.

Simon rang that night to ask me how I was, and then launched straight in to how brilliant his holiday was. So I told him how great my mum had been, being there for me when he wasn't, which made me feel better. She really was great. If I won the lottery I'd take *her* off on a holiday!

Simon came back from his holiday two weeks later and acted like nothing had happened. We split up a month later. I got fed up with us not being able to talk about anything and I couldn't handle the way he was with me.

I just want to say a great big thank you to my mum. If it wasn't for her I don't know how I would have got through all this.

I feel a lot better in myself now. I used to be 21 stone and I've lost some weight, so I feel a lot more confident than before. I've bought my own car and I'm going to start driving lessons. And I'm in a brilliant relationship now. I can't believe somebody loves me just the way I am. I am moving in with my boyfriend next month and he's doing everything in the flat to get it ready. We're planning a baby next year when we've saved enough money. The future is looking great.

Chantal Baker

Thank You

Although I'm single, my pregnancy was planned. I've always wanted to have children, ever since I can remember. I bought a home pregnancy test and sat in my bathroom peeing on the wand, knowing that in one minute's time I would find out whether or not I had a life growing inside me. A blue line appeared on the tester and the most amazing feeling filled me. I remember holding my tummy with my eyes shut and whispering 'thank you'.

I told my mum straight away. She was pleased for me as she knew it was what I had always wanted and that I wasn't stupid. She knew I would be able to look after and raise a child as well as any other mum, and I knew that I'd have her support. In this respect I was very lucky. A lot of people assumed that I wanted a child to make up for a lack of love in my childhood, but that wasn't true. It annoyed me to think that if I was married and 20 when I chose to have a baby, society would have found that acceptable.

I was totally spellbound by the whole experience. I remember my first scan at 12 weeks. The waiting room was packed with expectant mothers. My mum couldn't come and I didn't have a partner or even a friend with me, unlike everyone else. I didn't have a bump, so I had no obvious signs that I was pregnant. No one talked to me; they just stared. At this stage I wasn't aware of the prejudice that a single mum could come up against, especially if you are young.

When I saw the scan of the baby on the monitor, it was most beautiful thing that I had ever seen in my whole life. Tiny but perfect.

I finally started showing at around five months. People's reactions changed towards me once I had a bump. At the time I was doing a course in business administration so that I wouldn't just sit around doing nothing for nine months. It also meant that I would have a recognised qualification on top of my GCSEs, which would help me get a good job when the time came. The other teenagers at the college treated me as if I was a grown up trying to be 'young' and the adults treated me like a teenager trying to be 'grown up'. Both sides were very nice and all mothered me, but I didn't really feel as if I fitted in with either group. I wasn't into talking about boys and clubbing with the other teenagers, but I wasn't really into talking about washing powder and recipes with the adults, either. There was also a big part of me that suddenly had this massive responsibility to carry around for the rest of my life: would I be a good mum, would I teach the baby all the things it needed to know, would it suffer from not having a father, what would its future hold – the list was endless.

Antenatal classes were a total nightmare. There were seven or eight married couples and me. One woman went out of her way to involve me and make me feel welcome, but it just made me feel very out of place and patronised. I was determined to continue the classes as I felt it was important for my baby. I wanted to have as much information and advice as possible. My mum was very good in this department. We talked until the early hours of the morning some nights about things that were worrying me, or just about baby stuff in general. We were both very excited.

I got very emotional and temperamental when I was pregnant. I was prone to cry at Elvis songs or laugh uncontrollably at silly adverts on TV and I had backache, headaches, morning sickness, heartburn, trapped wind and a bladder that seemed to be on a 30-minute timer, 24 hours a day.

By the end of my pregnancy I looked like the back of a bus! I now had the waistline of Father Christmas and my stretch marks were making a road map of the entire planet over my tummy and my bum. I didn't really get upset by any of this, I was just amazed at the miracle of life. The fact that I had a tiny person growing inside me was the most wonderful, amazing experience and I absolutely loved it.

Labour was one experience that I don't think anyone can be totally prepared for. In a way you don't need to be because your body goes on automatic pilot. My waters broke on the Friday and by Saturday at 8.23 p.m. my baby, Theresa, was laid on my chest. My mum was crying, I was crying, and the baby just looked at both of us as if we were totally mad, not making a sound. I thought that it would feel strange or scary to finally see and hold the little person that I had made and carried for nine months, but it felt like the most natural thing in the world. I'd already bonded with the baby while I was pregnant and the moment I saw her the bond was sealed for ever. She was so amazing to me that I just lay awake all night, watching her sleep.

I had a lot of problems with breastfeeding, which upset me a great deal because it was something that I really wanted to do. The hospital were of no help at all. They treated me as if I was stupid and took it for granted that I wouldn't cope, but when I asked for help they didn't want to know. I don't think this attitude was solely based on my being a single mum; they seemed to treat everyone in a similar way.

I got the baby blues two days after Theresa was born. It was horrible. All I knew was that the world was about to end. I frequently burst into tears for no apparent reason and told everyone what a terrible mum I was going to be. It only lasted a couple of days, thank God!

The next two or three months were hard but enjoyable, although I don't think that I've ever been so tired in all my life! I cared for the baby, looked after her, taught her and clothed her. My mum would have helped in any way possible, but I wanted to be the one – even though to some I was too young – to do it all. It took me a few weeks to learn Theresa's patterns and to distinguish all her different cries, but I enjoyed every minute I spent with her. When I was tired or ill, or when she had the odd bad day and I felt like I was going mad, I would look at her and fall in love with her all over again.

Pregnancy and motherhood is like a worldwide club. From the moment your tummy begins to stick out, you get gooey-eyed looks from complete strangers. Unfortunately there is a minority that doesn't fit into this club – teenage mothers. Not only was I a teenage mum, but I had decided to do things on my own, so people seemed even more disapproving.

I still come up against prejudice. I remember having a conversation at a party with one woman. She seemed quite nice, but after about 10 minutes I mentioned Theresa and to my amazement she just turned away in the middle of my sentence, her smile fading to a disapproving scowl. I don't let it upset me any more. People only act this way towards me because of stereotypes. I've met teenage mums that aren't very good parents but I've also met 'grown-up' mums with a husband and a three-bedroom house who aren't very good parents. The main problems I get are when people see me as an age, not a person.

Soon after Theresa was born I set up my own Life Training Courses for teenagers (I'd been on a peer tutoring course with my local Brook before my pregnancy and gained valuable experience from them). My initial courses were on sex education. I felt that a lot of accidental pregnancies could be prevented with the power of knowledge; not just of how babies are made, but of contraception and relationships in general.

I went on many different training courses to get the right qualifications and then approached schools with my services. Once I got started it became obvious that there was a massive gap in the education system. I now also teach courses on HIV and AIDs, assertiveness and drug awareness. I don't lecture or judge anyone, I just talk and then let everyone else talk while I listen. In some cases the teenagers I work with feel that they can't talk to parents, teachers or even their friends, but they do learn valuable life information and skills from me that will help them to be in control of their own lives and their own futures.

I've been out socially about three times since Theresa was born. I could go out more, but I've never really been into getting 'slaughtered' and I also feel that as Theresa's mum, I should be in that role whenever she needs me. If anything, having her has given me the chance to do what I've always wanted: to be a mum and have a career.

I love every minute I spend with Theresa. I think she's taught me a lot even though she doesn't know it. I wonder what she'll be doing when she's 18. It could be anything, from a cleaner to a movie star. I don't care what she does, as long as she's happy and I just know that I'm going to enjoy sharing the next 17 years with her as we both find out.

Poppy Watkinson

It Wasn't Meant to Be

The day I found out I was pregnant my whole life fell apart. I was absolutely devastated. I was only just 18 and in the second year of my A levels. I had a place at university for October. My whole future was ahead of me.

My boyfriend and I were in the process of breaking up, so we weren't being very careful about contraception. I always thought it would never happen to me. My boyfriend was as shocked as I was when I told him and his first response was, 'Well, you can't keep it.' For some reason, we both laughed — not because it was funny but because it all seemed so serious and adult. I felt I was too young to have to deal with it.

We decided not to tell our parents and to organise an abortion as quickly as possible. I just wanted it all to go away, so my life could go back to normal. I told a few of my friends and somehow it became common knowledge.

My boyfriend's friends seemed to think it was funny and mine just thought it was something to gossip about. Pretty soon it got to the stage where we realised we would have to tell our parents as it was all too much.

We told my boyfriend's first and they took it really badly. They said what we planned to do was wrong and they got very upset. They wanted me to keep it. Mine reacted very differently. They were really angry at first, but so understanding in the end. Looking back, I don't know how I possibly thought I'd get through it without them. They agreed with my decision completely and tried to support me – even though they were disappointed.

It took about three weeks from having the pregnancy test until the abortion. By then, I was 10 weeks pregnant. During this time I had lots of different feelings about the baby. I knew I had to have an abortion. I had absolutely nothing to offer a child – no father, no money. There was so much I really wanted to do before I settled down. Despite this, I couldn't help thinking about whether it was a boy or girl and what it would look like. At the back of my mind, though, I knew I couldn't keep it and was fooling myself even considering anything else.

My boyfriend started to see someone else during these three weeks and became quite apathetic about it all. He told me I was over-reacting. This was so hard; I really needed him and he wasn't interested. Everyone, apart from my parents, seemed to think it was so easy and straightforward just to have an abortion.

On the day of the operation, I was very scared. In the ward every girl had someone with them. I was totally alone. The nurses left me on my own for ages while they dealt with the others. I can honestly say that was the lowest point of my whole life. I felt so lonely, as if no one understood, and the one person I really should have had with me just wasn't bothered.

When I went up to have the operation, I had to wait on a trolley in the corridor with another woman. She didn't seem at all fazed. The nurse waiting with us must have sensed I was anxious, because she started stroking my arm and telling me that 'it just wasn't meant to be'. She was right and I've always remembered those words ever since.

When I came round after the operation I just thought, What have I done? I started crying even though I was still drowsy from the anaesthetic. I had such regrets and this terrible pain in my stomach. The nurses were very busy and didn't have time to console me. They took me back to the ward for an hour and then I went home.

The next few days I stayed in bed. My mum looked after me so well, I couldn't have survived without her. I was an emotional wreck. My ex-boyfriend and my friends couldn't understand why I was so depressed. They kept telling me to pull myself together. In the end, things between me and my ex deteriorated and I told him to stop phoning me.

It wasn't until I started university and was able to get away that I felt properly happy for the first time. I didn't have any relationships for almost a year afterwards. I dreaded telling prospective boyfriends about the abortion; I thought they'd change their opinion of me. However, when I have felt it right to tell them, they've always tried to be sympathetic. It's such a big part of my past.

It's been two years now since the abortion. My parents

never mention it and my friends at home rarely do either. It still upsets me sometimes – especially when I see young women who are pregnant or hear of acquaintances who are having children. I sometimes feel that I took the easy way out and that I should have faced up to the consequences of my carelessness and had the baby. I often feel bitter that my boyfriend got away without even shedding a tear.

Most of the time I know I made the right decision. After all, I wouldn't be at university and have all the great friends and opportunities I have now if I hadn't had the termination. It was the right choice for me at the time, although it was one of the most awful experiences of my whole life.

When I do decide to have children I hope that I'll be a good mother and that I'll have something to offer them. In the meantime, I just want to focus on my degree and enjoy being young – the abortion has probably made me appreciate it more.

Liz Jenkins

A Pleasant Surprise

When I found out I was pregnant it came as a complete shock. I hadn't even suspected it – a friend asked me to accompany her to the clinic for a pregnancy test and I decided to have one too since my period was a little late. I wasn't in a stable relationship at the time, we were just having fun really. He was 17 and we'd been together for about 3 months. We did use contraception, but a condom had split once. I didn't really worry about it, until now...

When the nurse told me my test was positive, it didn't seem real. I was only 15 and had always assumed that things like this only happened to *other* people. Of course, my friend's test was negative. I think she was more shocked and panicky about my news than me! I spoke to the doctor at the clinic who was convinced that an abortion would be the best thing for me to do. I was quite taken aback by her attitude. She just expected me to go along with her advice and get rid of my baby!

When I got home I phoned another friend and told her about what had happened. She also thought I should have an abortion, but the more *I* thought about it, the more convinced I was that I wanted to keep the baby.

I felt like everyone was against me. I was intelligent and in the top classes at school, and my friends thought I was ruining my life. My boyfriend didn't seem all that concerned, but then I didn't really give him much of a chance to talk about it. I ended up saying I wanted to end the relationship. I was pretty horrible to him at the time, which I do regret now since he must have been as confused as I was.

By chance, in Biology the next week we were learning about reproduction and pregnancy, so my friends decided I should tell one of my teachers, and see what she thought. Looking back, I think my friends thought it was all very exciting, and didn't fully understand the implications of me having a baby so young, but I guess I didn't either. I actually put my teacher in rather a difficult position, since my mother worked at the same school and all the teachers knew her well. But she was very helpful and encouraged me to tell my mother, which was the hardest part for me. I knew Mum wouldn't be angry because I had a great relationship with her, but I didn't want to let her down. I plucked up the courage and told her in the car, on the way to the dentist's. She was great and asked me what I wanted to do. I told her I wanted to keep the baby and continue with my education and she said she'd support me all the way. I felt so relieved, like I wasn't on my own any more. Mum told my brothers who were rather nonchalant about the news and, finally, I told my dad over the phone (he works away). He was rather serious and came rushing up from London to talk to me. He was very nice though and talked me through my options and the implications of it all (like I hadn't already heard it a million times, but he meant well).

At school, it didn't take long for word to get round. All the kids were nice to me but I got very tired of having my stomach patted by people who normally wouldn't give me the time of day. The baby was due 3 July, and I had my GCSE exams in May and June, so I tried to concentrate on my work. Some of the teachers were okay, but a lot of them were quite negative, which I found difficult because I was feeling very happy and positive about my baby.

I was lucky because most of my pregnancy was very straightforward. I didn't start showing until over six months, I had no morning sickness and felt well throughout! It was at six months, when I was out with my friends, that a lad called Steven who I'd known for a couple of years told me he wanted to start seeing me. I was amazed – I'd already resigned myself to being a single mum for the rest of my life. I liked Steven too so I said yes, and we started dating. His parents weren't too pleased about it, although they were always polite to my face. I suppose it was understandable really, but I didn't feel very understanding when they were making life difficult for us. However, they came round eventually when they realised he was serious about me. Steven was fantastic all the way through the final months of my pregnancy. He acted like it was his own baby and kept me sane when I thought I couldn't cope.

I applied for college to do A levels and was

conditionally accepted. I chose a college with a crèche and put my baby down for a place. All I had to do was get through my GCSEs. This was made a lot easier by a scheme run by the local authority where pregnant girls go to a special school to study for their exams. I was quite apprehensive about this as it meant leaving all my friends, but I would be going to a school with other teenagers in the same position. I started there when I was about 28 weeks pregnant. I was picked up in the morning by the teacher (who was really wonderful) and taken back home at dinnertime (the school hours were only 10 till 12.30, Monday to Thursday). So I worked hard and sat my nine GCSEs at that school.

After the exams were out of the way, I had only three weeks to relax before the baby was due, so I made the most of it. I wasn't at all worried about the birth, as I'd read up on pain relief and decided on an epidural. I wanted Steven and my mum to be my birth partners and I knew that I would be well looked after. I took comfort in the fact that millions and millions of women had done this before me and told myself it would all be worth it in the end. When I was 38 weeks the doctor decided that due to a problem with the placenta, my baby was too small. So at 39 weeks I was induced. After an 11-hour labour, and an epidural that didn't work properly, I gave birth to a baby boy of 7 pounds 10 ounces. I didn't need stitches and recovered pretty well afterwards. I just looked at him and knew I'd done the right thing. It was all very emotional!

I was dying to take my baby Cameron home and look after him properly, and I came out after three days. Everyone was completely smitten with him, especially my mum and Steven, and I loved being a mum. In the first few months there were times when I thought I couldn't cope, but I've been incredibly lucky with the amount of help and support I've received from my family and friends. Cameron was a difficult baby, very colicky, and he used to cry for hours on end for no apparent reason. But he was worth all the effort and gives so much back in return.

I'm 18 now, and still very happy with my boyfriend. We're expecting a second baby in a few months' time. I'm nearing the end of my A level course and have my exams in about a month. I'm planning on taking a year out to spend with the children and then going on to university to study Business Management. I think being a teenage mother has made me much more mature and motivated. I feel happy with my life and lucky that I have such a wonderful son and family. As far as I'm concerned, I haven't missed out on anything. I still live with my mum, so I get to go out with my friends and have a good social life. Money isn't really a problem as my boyfriend has a good job and I don't have a house to run and pay for. My son is spoiled rotten by everybody and his real dad comes to see him every week.

I suppose if I were to talk about the downside of being a teenage mother, I would say that you do have to grow up quickly and miss out on your youth a bit. I don't get a lot of time to myself and definitely have more stress than the average 18-year-old girl. But as I said, for me, the benefits far outweigh the costs and I am confident that by keeping my baby I did the right thing.

Catherine Bennett

Contributors' Notes

Chantal Baker is now living with her boyfriend at his mum and dad's so they can save up for a home and start a family. She has a full-time job at a private day nursery, and feels that the future is looking great!

Julia Baynton has now trained as an air stewardess and really likes to travel and see new places. She also likes swimming and aerobics, reading and socialising with her family and friends.

Catherine Bennett now has a daughter aged one and works part-time in the Civil Service. She likes going out with her friends and listening to chart and dance music. She also likes trampolining and bowling.

Kim Black has achieved her ambition of becoming a junior secretary and wants to carry on up the ladder to success. She likes going out with her friends and spending too much money! She feels really happy about the future.

Lucy Bond really likes going out clubbing with friends and listening to soul music. She also likes drama and running, especially sprinting. Lucy says none of this would be possible without the support she gets from her mum with babysitting.

Jane Clark now lives with her mum and sister. She still enjoys every day with her daughter and is hoping to go back to work soon.

Rosy Cooper likes soul and garage music but feels she doesn't have much spare time to go out with her friends. Looking after her son is a full-time job!

Julie Cruickshank, who is now 22, lives with her boyfriend and two children. Daniel is now nearly five and at school and Robyn is two and a half and at playgroup. Family life doesn't really leave time for hobbies, but Julie likes to read and paint. When Robyn starts school, Julie hopes to find a job working with children.

Debbie Curran likes watching soaps and programmes where they film real life. She also enjoys chart music and comedy films. At the moment she is a guide leader. In the future she'd like to see more of the world and to get a job in accounts and finance. She hopes that one day her daughter will ask to see her.

Sara Earnshaw lives with her son Joe, four, and their cat, Dylan. She enjoys films, music and spending time with close friends. She has a boyfriend whom she loves very much and is looking forward to a positive future.

Mya Elmahelm really likes house and garage music and going clubbing with friends. She also enjoys action films and going out for meals. Her aim is to get a better education so that she can get a job and come off benefits.

Dawn Evans is totally into R&B, soul and hip hop. She loves clubbing with friends and travelling and keeps fit with kick boxing and aerobics.

Andrea Gardiner now lives with her son in a two-bedroomed, privately-rented house. She still visits the young women's support project where her son has a nursery place.

Claire-Marie Green now has a baby girl and is living with her boyfriend. She would love to have more children in the future. When she has spare time she likes doing cross stitch.

Rachel Griffiths likes swimming and reading lots of horror point books. She enjoys socialising with her friends and listening to chart music. At the moment she is doing a computer course and hopes to work with computers, maybe as a secretary.

Liz Jenkins is currently finishing her degree and hopes to go on and do a postgraduate course. She enjoys aerobics, football, shopping and socialising – and listening to Tori Amos, Garbage and Paul Weller. She would like to travel and work abroad.

Tanya Jones' time is mostly taken up with looking after her little girl, but she enjoys walking and beaches in her spare time. At the moment she is in college and doesn't have any solid plans for the future, but would like to work in animal welfare.

Marianne Lacey, or Maz, as her friends call her, lives with her son, Joshua. She is at college doing her GCSEs in English and Maths. In her spare time she loves spending time with Joshua and socialising with her friends.

Jayne Short spends most of her spare time with her children but she really enjoys her work as an independent advocate for young people who are or have been looked after by the local authority. The job brings so many challenges and rewards it's kind of like parenthood. She also plays netball and supports her oldest daughter in her love of Steps, Brittany Spears, and B'witched!

Helen Tomlinson likes to have a drink with friends in her spare time, and loves reading books by Jackie Collins. She hopes to go to college to study childcare.

Poppy Watkinson is very family orientated and likes to spend a lot of her time with her mum and daughter. She also gets a lot of pleasure from her work with teenagers and in the past has done a lot for TV and radio. Currently she's a DJ for the local hospital radio.

Samantha Williams now lives with her boyfriend in a Housing Association flat. They are looking for a flat nearer her mum so they can have more contact.

Due to the nature of this book, two of the contributors have asked their details to remain obscure.

Factfile

Q. Can I get contraception without my parents knowing?

A. Yes. Contraceptive advice is free and confidential. Even if you're under 16 your parents shouldn't be told without your permission.

Q. Where can I go to get contraception?

A. You can go to Brook, a family planning clinic or your GP for contraception. If you feel a bit embarrassed going to your family doctor, you can register with another GP for 'family planning only'.

Q. If I'm on the pill, does it matter if I miss one or two?

A. Yes. The pill is a really safe and effective contraceptive but only if you take it correctly. If you miss one, have a stomach upset, or take antibiotics, the pill may not work and you could get pregnant. This can happen even if you have been taking it for several years.

Q. *Is there anything I can do if I have sex without using contraception but I don't want to get pregnant?*

A. Yes. If you have unprotected sex you can get emergency (after sex) contraception from Brook, a family planning clinic or a GP. Emergency contraception works up to 72 hours after sex, but the sooner you take it the better.

Q. *Can I talk to a doctor about pregnancy without my parents knowing?*

A. Yes. Even if you're under 16 you can get a free and confidential pregnancy test at Brook and at most family planning clinics and GPs. Home tests are very accurate but quite expensive. If you are not sure what to do about the pregnancy, you can talk things through confidentially with a counsellor at Brook, a local youth counselling service or with your doctor.

Q. *If I don't want to continue the pregnancy, can I ask for an abortion?*

A. You can ask for an NHS abortion referral from Brook, a family planning clinic or GP. If you're under 16, it is legal to have an abortion without your parents knowing, but the doctor will strongly encourage you to involve them, or another adult, so you have some support. The legal limit for abortion is 24 weeks, although in very exceptional situations an abortion may be done later. If you are refused an abortion referral, call Brook (page 114) for advice.

Q. If I decide to have the baby and I'm still at school, do I have to leave?

A. Some schools think pregnancy is catching and may ask you to leave! Thankfully, not many do this any more and schools are being strongly encouraged to help any pupils who are pregnant to carry on with their studies. The Local Education Authority (LEA) has a legal duty to provide you with education up to 16, but this could range from a full-time place in a special unit for pregnant pupils to a few hours a week home tuition. If you're unhappy with what you're offered, take your case to the LEA or ring one of the Helplines (page 114) for advice.

Q. If I'm working, can I be sacked for being pregnant?

A. If you are sacked or chosen for redundancy because of your pregnancy, it is unlawful sex discrimination and automatically counts as an unfair dismissal. If this happens, it's important to get legal advice straight away. Phone The Maternity Alliance (page 114) for more information.

Resources

Brook
Free, confidential sex advice and contraception for young people. For your nearest centre call 0800 0185 023.

Childline
0800 1111

The Children's Legal Centre
Free and confidential legal advice and information for children and young people, 01206 873820.

FPA Contraceptive Education Service Helpline
Confidential contraceptive advice and details of local clinics, 0207 837 4044.

The Maternity Alliance
For advice on maternity benefits and employment rights, 0207 588 8582.